PLACES FOR TWO-YEAR-OLDS IN THE EARLY YEARS

Grounded in recent research on the challenges of working with two-year-olds, *Places for Two-year-olds in the Early Years* explores how this often overlooked age group is presented in policy and practice, and discusses why working with two-year-olds can be both exciting and highly rewarding. The book builds on theoretical understandings of child development, high-quality provision and pedagogical practice, to offer practical solutions to working effectively with two-year-olds and their families in a variety of early years settings.

Chapters focus on the specific needs of two-year-olds and the accompanying demands made on settings and practitioners. Many topics are also approached from a practical perspective, prompting readers to consider their own experiences of working with two-year-olds. The book explores:

* understandings of 'high-quality' education and care
* varying workforce requirements and professional development
* how practitioners develop knowledge(s) about working with two-year-olds
* physical and social environments for two-year-olds
* the role of the adult or key person in supporting children's development
* provision of services for disadvantaged two-year-olds.

With reflective questions and annotated further reading included throughout, *Places for Two-year-olds in the Early Years* is essential reading for practitioners, policy-makers and students involved in this often overlooked area of early years provision.

Jan Georgeson is Senior Research Fellow in Early Education Development at the Plymouth Institute of Education, Plymouth University, UK. She has a background in teaching young children with special educational needs.

Verity Campbell-Barr is Associate Professor in Early Childhood Studies at the Plymouth Institute of Education, Plymouth University, UK, and was until recently European Research Fellow in the Faculty of Child and Adult Education at the University of Debrecen, Hungary.

RESEARCH INFORMED PROFESSIONAL DEVELOPMENT FOR THE EARLY YEARS

TACTYC (Association for Professional Development in Early Years)

The books in this series each focus on a different aspect of research in early childhood which has direct implications for practice and policy. They consider the main research findings which should influence practitioner thinking and reflection and help them to question their own practice alongside activities to deepen knowledge and extend understanding of the issues. Readers will benefit from clear analysis, critique and interpretation of the key factors surrounding the research as well as exemplifications and case studies to illustrate the research-practice or research-policy links. Supporting the development of critical reflection and up-to-date knowledge, the books will be a core resource for all those educating and training early years practitioners.

Exploring the Contexts for Early Learning
Challenging the School Readiness Agenda
Rory McDowall Clark

Building Knowledge in Early Childhood Education
Young Children Are Researchers
Jane Murray

Early Childhood Education and Care for Sustainability
International Perspectives
Valerie Huggins and David Evans

Places for Two-Year-Olds in the Early Years
Supporting Learning and Development
Jan Georgeson and Verity Campbell-Barr

PLACES FOR TWO-YEAR-OLDS IN THE EARLY YEARS

Supporting Learning and Development

Edited by Jan Georgeson and Verity Campbell-Barr

LONDON AND NEW YORK

First published 2018
by Routledge
2 Park Square, Milton Park, Abingdon, Oxon OX14 4RN

and by Routledge
711 Third Avenue, New York, NY 10017

Routledge is an imprint of the Taylor & Francis Group, an informa business

© 2018 selection and editorial matter, Jan Georgeson and Verity Campbell-Barr, individual chapters, the contributors

The right of Jan Georgeson and Verity Campbell-Barr to be identified as the authors of the editorial material, and of the authors for their individual chapters, has been asserted in accordance with sections 77 and 78 of the Copyright, Designs and Patents Act 1988.

All rights reserved. No part of this book may be reprinted or reproduced or utilised in any form or by any electronic, mechanical, or other means, now known or hereafter invented, including photocopying and recording, or in any information storage or retrieval system, without permission in writing from the publishers.

Trademark notice: Product or corporate names may be trademarks or registered trademarks, and are used only for identification and explanation without intent to infringe.

British Library Cataloguing in Publication Data
A catalogue record for this book is available from the British Library

Library of Congress Cataloging in Publication Data
A catalog record for this book has been requested

ISBN: 978-1-138-18528-9 (hbk)
ISBN: 978-1-138-18529-6 (pbk)
ISBN: 978-1-315-64458-5 (ebk)

Typeset in Bembo
by Out of House Publishing

CONTENTS

Acknowledgements	*vii*
Contributors	*viii*
Preface by Janet Moyles and Jane Payler	*xi*

1 Introduction
Verity Campbell-Barr and Jan Georgeson
    1

2 The minding of two-year-olds
Rod Parker-Rees
    8

3 Vulnerable identities
Anita Soni
    23

4 Quality for two-year-olds
Verity Campbell-Barr
    36

5 Talking about two-year-olds: The potential impact of
early years discourses on identity formation
Gill Boag-Munroe
    50

6 Ways of working with two-year-olds
Jan Georgeson
    63

7 Qualifications, knowledge and preparedness for working
with two-year-olds
Verity Campbell-Barr
    75

vi Contents

8 Different places for two-year-olds 93
Jan Georgeson

9 Environments for listening 103
Karen Wickett

10 Inspiring work with birth-to-twos: A creative and
cultural perspective 120
Clare Halstead

11 Working with two-year-olds: The role of Educational
Psychologist 135
Anita Soni

12 Concluding thoughts: What matters for high-quality
experiences for two-year-olds in early years settings? 142
Carmen Dalli

Index *151*

ACKNOWLEDGEMENTS

We would like to thank TACTYC not only for funding the *Two-year-olds in England* research which lies at the heart of this book, but also for their advice and patience during the course of the project.

We also acknowledge the work of our co-researchers on the *Two-year-olds in England* project; two have contributed to this book (Rod Parker-Rees and Gill Boag-Munroe) and Sandra Mathers helped with the overall design, report writing and led the national practitioner survey. We'd like to thank Federico Caruso who contributed to the compilation of the case studies and Julie Fletcher for help with the literature review. As ever, we are indebted to Mark Georgeson and Matt Monks for their timely support with proofreading, transcribing and tea. ·

Finally, we are deeply grateful to the practitioners who welcomed us into their settings, to stakeholders who answered our questions thoughtfully and to the children who invited us into their play.

CONTRIBUTORS

Gill Boag-Munroe is the tutor on the Master's in Learning and Teaching at the Department of Education, University of Oxford, initially in the English strand and now in the Generic strand, having previously taught on the PGCE course. She was part of the research teams that carried out the National Evaluation of the Early Learning Parenting Partnerships and the *Two-year-olds in England* project funded by TACTYC. Gill's research interests lie in hard-to-reach families and how educational establishments might reach out to them; and in identity construction in schools. With Jan Georgeson, she has explored the ways in which a systemic functional linguistic approach can assist in describing how early years practitioners construct identities for themselves and the children and families they work with, through the ways in which they decorate, furnish and sign their settings.

Verity Campbell-Barr is Associate Professor in Early Childhood Studies at the Plymouth Institute of Education, Plymouth University. She has recently completed a cross-European project on *Knowledge, Skills and Attitudes for the Early Childhood Education and Care Workforce*, funded by the European Commission. Her European work builds on her interest in quality early childhood education and care and the role of the workforce within this. Verity is co-author of *Quality and Leadership in the Early Years* with Dr. Caroline Leeson (published by Sage, UK) and has written extensively on the quality of early years services. Verity is an expert adviser for the European Commission, a Trustee for the British Association for Early Education and a part of the Early Childhood Workforce Initiative (coordinated by R4D and the International Step by Step Association).

Carmen Dalli is Professor of Early Childhood Education and Director of the Institute for Early Childhood Studies at the Faculty of Education at Victoria University of Wellington, New Zealand. Her research combines an interest in developmental issues in the early years with a focus on early childhood policy and pedagogy. She has published widely in the field of early childhood teacher professionalism and has a particular interest in group-based early childhood education and care settings for children aged under three years. She is co-editor, with E. Jayne White, of a new book series (Springer) entitled *Policy and Pedagogy with Under-three Year Olds: Cross-disciplinary Insights and Innovations.*

Jan Georgeson is Senior Research Fellow in Early Education Development at the Plymouth Institute of Education, Plymouth University and has a background in teaching young children with special educational needs. Later she was involved in supporting candidates for Early Years Professional Status from the pilot phase onwards and has edited books on professional development for early years practitioners. Her research interests currently include multiagency working, advocacy and inclusion, and European perspectives on professional development to support children's learning in mathematics and computer programming. Her research is strongly influenced by sociocultural and activity theory, in particular when applied to organisational structure, interactional style and approaches to pedagogy. She is co-editor of *Early Years: An International Research Journal* (with Rod Parker-Rees and Pamela Oberhuemer) and co-convenor of the BERA Early Childhood Education and Care Special Interest Group.

Clare Halstead has developed creative learning projects for people of all ages including under-fives for over 20 years. She has worked as a local authority arts officer, with Creative Partnerships, as a freelance artist and project manager and as Head of Learning at the Towner Gallery in Eastbourne. Based in Brighton, she is currently developing a new creative hub in Worthing and has recently become a Fellow of the Royal Society of Arts.

Rod Parker-Rees worked as a teacher with three- to five-year-old children before joining Plymouth University where he led a large Early Childhood Studies team. He is a co-editor (with Pamela Oberhuemer and Jan Georgeson) of *Early Years: An International Research Journal*. His writing is focused on playfulness and early, preverbal communication, and he has edited *Meeting the Child in Steiner Kindergartens: An Exploration of Beliefs, Values and Practices* (Routledge, 2011) and co-edited *Early Years Education (Major Themes in Education)* (Routledge, 2007) and *Early Childhood Studies: An Introduction to the Study of Children's Worlds and Children's Lives* (4th edn. Sage, 2015).

Anita Soni currently works as an independent educational psychologist working with clusters of children's centres and primary schools in the West Midlands. She has recently read and commented on early drafts of *Development Matters for the Early Years Foundation Stage* (Early Education, 2012) prior to publication. Anita is particularly interested in children's personal, social and emotional development, the Key Person approach, the use of group supervision with professionals from the children's workforce and supporting children with English as an additional language. Anita also works at the University of Birmingham as a tutor on the Educational Psychology programme.

Karen Wickett is the joint BA Early Childhood Studies programme lead at Plymouth University. Originally she qualified as an NNEB (National Nursery Examination Board) and later trained as an early years teacher. Between 2003 and 2012 she worked in a Sure Start Local Programme/Children's Centre (SSCC). During 2008 and 2012 she worked part-time in the SSCC and part-time at Plymouth University. One of her aims, as a part-time lecturer and children's centre teacher, was to narrow the divide between practice and theory. In 2010 she embarked on her Professional Doctorate in Education (EdD) and successfully completed her thesis in 2016. Her doctoral research explored the relationships and beliefs of parents, ECEC practitioners and teachers as they prepared and supported children during the transition to school. Karen's other research interests include learning in both formal and informal contexts and creativity in the early years.

PREFACE

Professor Emerita Janet Moyles and Professor Jane Payler

Volume Four: *Places for Two-year-olds in the Early Years*

Welcome to the fourth volume in the inspiring TACTYC book series. As part of the Association for Professional Development in Early Years, TACTYC members believe that effective early years policies and practices should be informed by an understanding of the findings and implications of high-quality, robust research. TACTYC focuses on developing the knowledge base of all those concerned with early years education and care by creating, reviewing and disseminating recent, cutting-edge research findings and by encouraging critical and constructive discussion to foster reflective attitudes in practitioners. Such a need has been evident in the resounding success of events such as our conferences where speakers make clear connections between research and practice for delegates. Early years practitioners and those who support their professional development engage enthusiastically with research and understand how it is likely to impact upon, and enhance, practice. They acknowledge that research has a distinct role to play in effective work in early years education and care, and that they should be part of a research-rich education system.

TACTYC is an organisation with a specific focus on the professional development of all those involved in early childhood with the express purpose of improving practices to enhance the well-being of young children. Its reputation for quality research and writing includes its international journal, *Early Years*. The TACTYC book series will appeal to those who value the journal as it complements its range and scope. Our aim for the series is to help those who educate and train early years practitioners at all levels to access recent research, to highlight the professional development implications and to offer a rationale for improving the quality and reach of practice in early years education and care.

The claim is frequently made that policies are 'evidence-based', but this is not the same as rigorous, impartial research. Many policy and practice documents purport to be based on 'evidence', but this depends to a large extent on the political framework and ideology in place at different periods in time. Few governments have the scope in their relatively short elected periods to give strategic consideration to the complex implications of different research outcomes for policies and practice. What is politically and economically expedient at the time is too often the driving force behind decisions about young children and their families.

In 2013, the TACTYC Executive felt driven to call for and fund research into the realities and complexities of early childhood education and care (ECEC) for two-year-olds as a direct response to an English policy initiative. The policy appeared to imply that 'disadvantaged' two-year-olds could be easily identified and their lives rapidly improved by offering funded access to ECEC, much of which had been developed in services appropriate for older children. It appeared that there was insufficient consideration of the challenges inherent in such a policy for both those providing services and those using them. As Campbell-Barr and Georgeson so neatly describe in their introduction to this volume, two-year-olds constitute 'a forgotten age group, sandwiched between research into early education for children aged three years to school age and developmental research on babies'. Our deep concern in calling for research was to understand the experiences of the two-year-olds, their families and the practitioners who worked with them. We hoped to be able to shed light on the realities of living alongside, caring for and educating two-year-old children in expanding services. From this, we hoped to promote deeper considerations of what effective pedagogy and effective services could look like and to highlight the professional development and support needs of practitioners.

Places for Two-year-olds is primarily inspired by that funded study, *Two-year-olds in England*, which was carried out by Jan Georgeson and colleagues at Plymouth University and Oxford University. The book does not disappoint. It combines findings from that and other research with broader considerations of theory, international policy and practice, before drawing conclusions about what matters most from the overarching themes of relationships, environments and infrastructure. Time constraints can make it a challenge for busy trainers and practitioners to access contemporary research and translate it into informed and reflective practice. The book offers everyone the opportunity to become more fully informed and to reflect more deeply on issues relating to the care and education of two-year-olds.

About the book series

All the writers in this series have been asked to present their particular focus, and to outline the issues and challenges within that framework which are relevant for early years practitioners. Exploring aspects of early years practice, based on research and sound theoretical underpinning, each of the writers offers guidance on how findings can be analysed and interpreted to inform the continuing process of developing high-quality early years practice. They will examine the research background to each topic and offer considered views on why the situation is as it is, and how it might move forward within imposed frameworks of curricula and assessments. They offer thoughtful advice to practitioners for dealing with the challenges faced within that particular focus and suggest relevant follow-up reading and web-based materials to support further reflection, practice and curriculum implementation. Each book also identifies where further research is needed and will help tutors, trainers and practitioners to understand how they can contribute to research in this field.

Early childhood education and care is universally contentious, especially in relation to how far those outside the field, e.g. politicians and policy-makers, should intervene in deciding what constitutes successful early years pedagogy, curriculum and assessment. The main focus of the series is on practice, policy and provision in the UK, but writers will also draw on international research perspectives as there is a great deal to learn from colleagues in other national contexts.

The series particularly targets readers qualified at Level 6, or students on such courses, preparing for roles in which they will be expected to educate and train other practitioners in effective early years practices. There will be many others who will find the books invaluable: leaders of early years settings, who often have an education, training and professional development role in relation to their staff (and may well be qualified at Level 6 or beyond) will similarly find the series useful in their work. Academics and new researchers who support the training and development of graduate leaders in early years will also appreciate the books in this series. Readers will benefit from clear analysis, critique and interpretation of the key factors surrounding the research, together with exemplifications and case studies to illustrate the links between research and policy as well as research and practice. The books will support the development of critical reflection and up-to-date knowledge, and will be a core resource for all those educating and training early years practitioners.

In summary, research-based early years practice is a relatively new field as much of practitioners' work with young children over recent years, particularly in England, has been based on the implementation of policy documents, which are often not grounded in rigorous, clear, unambiguous research evidence. The main aim of the TACTYC series is to help tutors and trainers to enable practitioners to become more informed advocates for provision of high-quality services for children and their families. This will be achieved by promoting the benefits of applying research in an informed way to improve quality. We hope readers find much in the fourth book of the series to inspire their reflections, training and practice.

1

INTRODUCTION

Verity Campbell-Barr and Jan Georgeson

The provision of early education services for children prior to entering school has an established history in many parts of the world, well illustrated in European countries by early education pioneers, such as Montessori, Froebel and McMillan. More recently, supra-national organisations such as the World Bank and European Commission have identified the importance of early education services for providing the foundations for children's lifelong learning, whilst offering early intervention to support equality of opportunity amongst children irrespective of socio-economic status. Increased interest in early education services for supporting children's holistic development has led to increased scrutiny, ranging from analysis of staffing requirements and pedagogical approaches to consideration of the age at which children should access early education.

Traditionally, early education services have been associated with provision for children from the age of three to statutory school age, and have been divided from care services for young children. Divided models are associated with different pedagogical traditions, disjointed policy objectives and inequality of experiences for children, potentially making transitions more difficult for children as they move into school (Moss, 2006; Lindeboom and Buiskool, 2013). More integrated models that adopt a holistic approach towards services for children from birth to school age are regarded as more favourable. Whilst there are challenges to creating a holistic model (Moss, 2006), moves towards a more holistic approach have revealed that far more is known about working with children from the age of three to school age than with younger children. In particular, two-year-olds appear to be a forgotten age group, sandwiched between research into early education for children aged three to school age and developmental research on babies. This book therefore aims to bring together theoretical perspectives, empirical research and practical examples of two-year olds in the places where they receive education and care.

2 Verity Campbell-Barr and Jan Georgeson

The origins of the book's focus on two-year-olds in early education services and our own explorations of services for two-year-olds were prompted by two related issues. The first was that the Department for Education introduced free early education places for disadvantaged two-year-olds in England. The second was, given the comparative lack of research on this age group, what does early education for two-year-olds mean in practice? There have been universal free early education places for three- and four-year-olds available since 2010 (with a phased introduction of funded places from 1997 providing an even longer history of provision). This meant that early years practitioners were experienced at working with three- and four-year-olds, but there was no certainty that this experience could be transferred to working with two-year-olds. A further complexity is that, whilst early education places in England are an entitlement funded by the state, these places are delivered by a mixed economy of providers. Private, voluntary, independent and state services could all offer free early education places through drawing down government funding. Extending funding to offer places to disadvantaged two-year-olds might have appeared straightforward but for several reasons this was not the case.

The mixed economy of service provision, involving private, voluntary, independent (PVI) and maintained sector providers, posed a number of potential challenges. Firstly, some providers had little or no history of working with two-year-olds and/ or practitioners' training had not focused on work with two-year-olds. For example, those working in maintained nurseries or in primary schools tend to have experience of working with children from three years of age, but not younger. In addition, initial training for those in the maintained sector, although at degree level, often focused on working with children from three years of age (if not older), indicating potential gaps in the knowledge base of staff members in this sector. Furthermore, in response to evidence that it was high-quality early education that would most benefit disadvantaged children, the free places were to be offered by settings that had achieved the highest-quality standards in government inspections. For settings with no history of working with two-year-olds, this inspection had to be based on services for three- and four-year-olds. Research has, however, indicated that whilst government quality standards are associated with other quality indicators for three- and four-year-olds, the associations with quality for two-year-olds are less clear (Mathers et al., 2012). This means that, although the intention of the funding initiative was that the funded two-year-old places would be provided by the highest-quality settings, the targeting processes could not guarantee that this was the highest quality for two-year-olds. For example, consideration of practical issues such as the provision for toilet training and space for nap times shows that the needs of two-year-olds are different from those of three- and four-year-olds.

There was the potential therefore that the maintained sector might be less well placed to offer places for two-year-olds, particularly when compared with the private, voluntary and independent sectors that had a history of offering full daycare alongside early education for children as young as three months to school age. However, despite being more experienced, the PVI sectors were not required to have the degree-level training present in the maintained sector (see Chapter 7).

Furthermore, there were already indications that those who worked with children under the age of three tended to be the lowest qualified staff (Norris, 2010; Mathers et al., 2011; Goouch and Powell, 2013) and, whilst there are degree-qualified staff in the PVI sectors, they were not necessarily working with two-year-olds. There were therefore concerns that the early education that was to be provided for two-year-olds might lead to experiences of variable quality.

Finally, further challenges arose because the funded places were to be targeted at 'disadvantaged' two-year-olds, with eligibility defined by the same income and benefits criteria used for free school meals. Staff working in settings offering places for two-year-olds therefore needed to be particularly skilled and knowledgeable in order to support children likely to be at greater risk of having additional needs and/or developmental delay and contribute information on children's (dis)abilities to complete a check on their progress. Previous evaluations of the two-year-olds offer (Smith et al., 2009; Gibb et al., 2011) have shown that these extra needs require extra resources.

The questions posed, both practically and pedagogically, by the provision of early education for two-year olds led to TACTYC commissioning a piece of research to consider what high-quality early education for two-year-olds might look like and what was happening in practice as the funded places initiative unfolded. The research involved a literature review, interviews with experts, a survey of practitioners and a series of case studies that included observations of practice and interviews with staff about working with two-year-olds (Georgeson et al., 2014). Chapters in this book draw on different stages of the research and are supplemented by chapters that expand on important themes that emerged from the analysis and offer examples of practice. Whilst common themes run through the book, readers will encounter different perspectives and approaches designed to prompt them to consider their own personal perspective on working with two-year-olds.

The book begins with a series of more theoretical chapters. The first two – 'The minding of two-year-olds' by Rod Parker-Rees and 'Vulnerable identities' by Anita Soni – illustrate both common themes and different perspectives that emerged when we explored working with two-year-olds. Both chapters consider child development, but from different theoretical perspectives. In Chapter 2, Rod Parker-Rees encourages readers to consider how children make sense of their worlds. The use of 'minds' is less about the mind in a neurological sense than about minding in a pedagogical sense, whereby those who work with young children share interests and interact with children. The chapter therefore enables the reader to consider how shared interests can be developed between an adult and a child and how an adult may then extend this interest to support children's development. The chapter is written from socio-cultural perspectives and is focused on children's development. In Chapter 3, Anita Soni similarly explores child development and the role of the adult within this, but concentrates on the interplay between disadvantage and vulnerability and children's development. Awareness of the importance of early intervention can be traced back to strong messages emerging from the psychology literature and this chapter focuses on

4 Verity Campbell-Barr and Jan Georgeson

the idea of critical stages of development and on established theories of attachment and their implications for those working with young children. Anita develops the chapter to consider research into vulnerable and disadvantaged groups who might access early education services and the development of identity and resilience. The ensuing discussion of risk and protective factors offers a more complex view of disadvantage and vulnerability to avoid the slide into assumptions about the lives of those who are raised in poverty or who experience other difficulties. The chapter then returns to the subject of attachments to explore the Key Person role within early education settings.

The connection to policy is continued in Verity Campbell-Barr's chapter on 'Quality for two-year-olds' (Chapter 4), where she outlines policy interest and developments in early education services in England. The chapter focuses on the government's decision to provide early education places for disadvantaged two-year-olds and how this was steeped in the much-debated concept of quality. The chapter includes a consideration of different theoretical perspectives on quality, asking who and what informs understandings of quality and how such ideas can have implications for the ways in which early education services are understood and discussed. The chapter then continues by considering empirical research to explore what might be distinct about high-quality early education for two-year-olds. The chapter identifies different aspects of quality, such as the workforce and working with parents, providing the foundations for later chapters in the book.

In Chapter 5, Gill Boag-Munroe is also concerned with who and what shapes understandings, but this time focusing on how language shapes understandings about two-year-olds. In Chapter 2, Parker-Rees discussed how two-year-olds 'harvest' cultural information through 'paying attention to the way other people respond to things'; Boag-Munroe is concerned with how two-year-olds pay attention to the way other people respond to them. The chapter includes consideration of the language of policy but also considers how the language of a popular text – illustrated by terms such as 'terrible twos' – is used to describe two-year-olds and shape both what adults understand about two-year-olds and how two-year-olds begin to understand who they are. Through the exploration of international literature, Gill highlights the cultural construction of two-year-olds and the care needed to avoid transmitting societal negativity about the age group to their developing minds.

In Chapter 6, Jan Georgeson builds on the earlier chapters to consider what pedagogy might look like for two-year-olds. The chapter focuses specifically on the concept of watchfulness, drawing on empirical research with those working in early education settings with two-year-olds to consider how staff engage in interactions with two-year-olds to enact a relational pedagogy. The chapter explores how those working with two-year-olds anticipate and respond to children's actions in order to interact with them sensitively. The chapter draws attention to both the complexities and intricacies of working with young children, whilst recognising the factors that can influence an assessment of whether an individual is identified as being 'good' at working with two-year-olds. Making connections to earlier chapters, Georgeson considers the different influences, such as the views of managers and colleagues, that mould the degree of professional autonomy for an individual working with children in a setting. This focus on the practice of working with two-year-olds acts as a bridge into the next section of the book, where the chapters have a more practical focus.

To provide some context to considering the practice of working with two-year-olds, Chapter 7, 'Qualifications, knowledge and preparedness for working with two-year-olds' by Verity Campbell-Barr begins by considering who works with two-year-olds and the varying workforce requirements that exist. The chapter examines the importance of the initial training of those who will work in early years education, and draws on both international literature and empirical research to consider whether people feel prepared for working in early education. The empirical research relates directly to the funding of places for two-year-olds and establishes that, whilst initial training provides a general feeling of preparedness for working with children from birth to the age of five, staff report feeling less prepared for working specifically with two-year-olds or for some of the challenges that can come with working with children from disadvantaged backgrounds. The chapter connects with the previous chapter in seeking to identify the challenges of working with two-year-olds, presenting the notion of considering knowledge in the plural – knowledges – in order to illustrate the rich and varied ways people come to know how to work with young children. Chapter 8 by Jan Georgeson also illustrates the complexities of knowing how to work with two-year-olds by offering a series of case studies showing who is working with two-year-olds, where and how. The chapter provides real examples from contexts visited during the *Two-year-olds in England* research project and explores the approach to working with two-year-olds in each setting from the perspective of those who work there.

Chapters 9, 10 and 11 continue the focus on practice, offering inspirational examples of the different ways in which services can be provided for two-year-olds. In Chapter 9, Karen Wickett explores the challenges and rewards of introducing more open spaces into early education settings. The chapter traces the experiences of different early education settings that considered the physical structure of the buildings where they worked and the consequences that this had for both staff and children in the setting. The physicality of a wall is illustrated as offering both a physical and metaphorical barrier, whereby children's transitions and staff's identities are bounded by the structures of baby rooms and preschool rooms. Knocking down walls between different rooms is symbolic of knocking down the barriers that can limit children from deciding on their own transitions or that can make staff feel marginalised. Exploring spaces for two-year-olds is also present in Chapter 10, where Clare Halstead provides an overview of an innovative project to introduce the arts to two-year-olds and their families. The chapter provides an honest account of the tensions faced when seeking to open up art spaces for two-year-olds, whilst also identifying the rewards. In particular, the chapter identifies how physical spaces can act as supportive structures for children's learning, whilst the addition of interesting resources can provide children with a wealth of exploratory experiences. In Chapter 11, Anita Soni offers a different perspective on working with

6 Verity Campbell-Barr and Jan Georgeson

two-year-olds by sharing how, as an educational psychologist, she is able to offer support and guidance to parents and families of two-year-olds.

In the final chapter, Carmen Dalli brings an international perspective to working with two-year-olds, by contextualising the growth of participation by under-twos in group-based early childhood provision across OECD countries. From her reading of the chapters, Carmen focuses on overarching messages about what matters: (i) relationships with knowledgeable, responsive adults; (ii) the physical environment and structural elements of quality (adult:child ratios as the preconditions for other quality characteristics); (iii) a supportive policy infrastructure.

A note on terminology

Throughout the book we have chosen to use early childhood education and care (ECEC) to refer to the services for two-year olds, not only because this is an internationally recognised term, but also as it brings together both education and care. Government initiatives in the UK have clouded understandings of care and education for many years. Whilst there have been attempts to develop an educare model that represents the holistic approach of services for children from birth to school age, the historical divide between services is still evident. Most recently, the confusion in understanding between care and education has been evident in the use of 'early education' to refer to the free funded places, but a more general use of 'childcare' in policy proposals. Explorations of the distinction between early education and childcare are well rehearsed (Baldock et al., 2005; Moss, 2006; Campbell-Barr and Leeson, 2016), particularly for the implications for how services are understood, whereby care is associated with supporting parents to enter employment and education is about child development. Yet such distinctions create narrow conceptualisations of services; at the very least care is not devoid of education and vice versa. The use of ECEC is therefore about a more holistic construction of services and their role.

We have also used the terms 'practitioner' and 'staff' to refer in general to people who work with two-year-olds. We acknowledge that this includes a whole range of job titles (teacher, nursery nurse, nursery assistant, nursery officer, room leader) that relate to the wide range of qualifications held by those working with this age range. Because of the strong message from people we interviewed in settings that there was something beyond qualifications that was needed to be 'good with two-year-olds', we have avoided using terms tied too closely to particular qualifications.

References

Baldock, P., Fitzgerald, D., and Kay, J. (2005). *Understanding Early Years Policy*, London: Paul Chapman.

Campbell-Barr, V., and Leeson, C. (2016). *Quality and Leadership in the Early Years*, London: Sage.

Georgeson, J., Campbell-Barr, V., Mathers, S., Boag-Munroe, G., Parker-Rees, R., and Caruso, F. (2014). *Two-year-olds in England: An exploratory study*. Available at: http://tactyc.org.uk/wp-content/uploads/2014/11/TACTYC_2_year_olds_Report_2014.pdf. (Accessed on: 09/09/2017)

Gibb, J., Jelicic, H., La Valle, I., Gowland, S., Kinsella, R., Jessiman, P., and Ormston, R. (2011). *Rolling out free early education for disadvantaged two-year-olds: An implementation study for local authorities and providers*. DFE-RR131, London: DfE.

Goouch, K., and Powell, S. (2013). Orchestrating professional development for baby room practitioners: Raising the stakes in new dialogic encounters. *Journal of Early Childhood Research*, 11(1): 78–92.

Lindeboom, G. and Buiskool, J. (2013). Quality in early childhood education and care. European Parliament. Directorate-General for Internal Policies. Policy Department B. Structural and Cohesion Policies, Culture and Education. Available at: www.europarl.europa.eu/studies. (Accessed on: 09/08/2017)

Mathers, S., Ranns, H., Karemaker, A., Moody, A., Sylva, K., Graham, J., and Siraj-Blatchford, I. (2011). *Evaluation of the graduate leader fund. Final report*. London: DfE. Available at: www.education.gov.uk/publications/standard/publicationDetail/Page1/DFE-RR144. (Accessed on: 09/08/2017)

Mathers, S., Singler, R., and Karemaker, A. (2012). *Improving quality in the early years: A comparison of perspectives and measures*, London: University of Oxford, Daycare Trust and A+ Education. Available at: www.education.ox.ac.uk/research/fell/research/improving-quality-in-the-early-years/. (Accessed on: 01/08/2017)

Moss, P. (2006). Farewell to childcare? *National Institute Economic Review*, 195 (1), 70–83

Norris, D. J. (2010). Raising the educational requirements for teachers in infant toddler classrooms: Implications for institutions of higher education. *Journal of Early Childhood Teacher Education*, 31, 146–158.

Smith, R., Purdon, S., Schneider, V., La Valle, I., Wollney, I., Owen, R., Bryson, C., Mathers, S., Sylva, K., and Lloyd, E. (2009). *Early education pilot for two-year-old children: Evaluation*. Research Report for DCSF No. RR134. London: Department for Children, Schools and Families.

2

THE MINDING OF TWO-YEAR-OLDS

Rod Parker-Rees

Introduction

The purpose of this chapter is to encourage people who will play a part in the minding of two-year-olds to reconsider our understanding of how young children notice and make sense of their world. By focusing on the *minding* of two-year-olds, rather than their minds, I hope to contribute to a shift in understanding, from thinking about children in terms of what they have *acquired* or *developed* to noticing how they are encouraged and enabled to *participate* in social communities.

This chapter will offer an exploration of the inextricably *social* nature of 'minding', particularly as this informs our thinking about how we can support two-year-olds as they move out from the familiar, private context of home and family into the more public world of early childhood education and care settings.

Minds and minding

I want to stretch the use of the word 'minding' beyond its conventional use. We have come to separate the idea of 'mind', as a noun, from the many ways in which we use 'mind' as a verb ('mind out!' 'Do you mind!' 'mind you ...' 'mind your own business' ...) but I want to play with three related ways in which 'minding' can be understood:

- **Minding is what minds do.** We have become used to thinking in terms of people *having* minds but this tends to hide the fact that minding is a process, and a shared process at that. It really makes no more sense to say that I have my 'own' mind than to say that I have my own conversations, interactions or even my own language. When we shift our attention from children's minds to children's minding, it becomes easier to recognise that this refers to the process of directing and focusing attention, both in social contexts and in 'private' thought.

- **Minding is the intentional sharing of ways of minding.** This sense can be understood by comparison with verbs like 'feeding' and 'clothing'. To feed or clothe someone is to offer what they need in order to be fed or clothed and while these terms can refer to the process of putting food in someone's mouth or putting clothes on their body, they can also refer to the less intimate process of making food and clothes available so that recipients can feed or clothe themselves. In a similar way, minding can be understood as the *pedagogical* process of intentionally sharing interests and attention with others, deliberately helping them to participate in the minding practices of a particular culture.
- **Minding is looking after or caring for something or someone.** This is the more familiar sense associated with what a childminder does. While it is often related to the first sense of minding (we expect childminders to focus their attention on the children they are minding), it can also have a rather pejorative sense akin to 'babysitting' or looking after animals. When understood in this way, minding may have connotations of 'just' responding to needs; an outdated and inaccurate association which is vigorously challenged by childminder organisations.

The focus of this chapter will be mainly on the second of these – how interactions with carers such as parents, grandparents, siblings, friends and neighbours 'scaffold' and support the minding of two-year-olds. How do we enable children to find out about what matters to us (both as individuals *and* as representatives of a shared culture) and how can we show *our* interest in what matters to them? How can we equip children with the public, cultural resources (including language but also less explicit ways of expressing values and beliefs) which will enable them to share their private interests with others; to 'make up their minds' and also to learn what other people mind about? I will argue that minding children in this active, intentional way can best be understood in terms of sharing meaning – indeed, meaning and minding have much in common:

> Sharing the meaning of experience appears to be a unique motivation of human cognition incorporating the intertwined motivations of making sense and making relationships.
>
> (Nelson, 2007: 17)

I will begin by outlining the early stages of learning to share attention. Noticing what people notice, and how they respond, leads, usually by the end of the first year, to an interest in the relationships between people and things or events; what things *mean* to particular people. This early awareness of differences in other people's minding enables infants to begin to separate various 'you's from the "Great We'" (Vygotsky, 1998: 232) of their first interactions and this also leads to the discovery of a self, initially perceived through the attention of other people.

Sharing experience and meanings with others allows children to become increasingly aware of patterns in how other people can be expected to feel about things. Noticing, sharing and sometimes contesting the mindings of others (and particularly of others who have an active interest in supporting them) helps children to develop skilful and culturally attuned management of their own minding. Becoming a member of a community involves learning how we are expected to fillet our experience – separating what is worth keeping, what we think will be interesting to other people, from what needs to be cut away/edited out or ignored, either because it is uninteresting, bland or useless, or because it may be offensive, irritating or disgusting.

Our minding, how we direct our attention, is both our own and not our own. To be able to share experiences and relationships we need to acknowledge the interests and mindings of others as well as to allow others (and ourselves) to get to know what is distinctive about us. The social negotiation of attention requires a complex to-ing and fro-ing between a child's 'own' interests and concerns and those of the people with whom these meanings and mindings are shared. Children internalise knowledge about other people's relationships with their environment (what they like, care about, etc.) but they also externalise their own understanding of what they have observed, in their uniquely modulated responses, imitations, play, utterances and, in time, in their speech. Internalised values and judgements allow us to observe and evaluate our own externalisations, to see ourselves as others see us.

For both two-year-olds and their interaction partners, sharing understanding depends on a shared awareness of the child's particular context. Familiarity with a shared world and a shared past allows familiar adults to 'know where a child is coming from', making them more able to 'scaffold' the child's minding. John Shotter (2012) uses the term 'withness thinking' to describe this intensely 'present' way in which thinking and minding can be situated in, and supported by, the features of a context outside our heads. Shotter contrasts 'withness thinking' with 'aboutness thinking' – the ability (and habit) of lifting ourselves out of our immediate context so that we can think 'about' it rather than 'in' it. Perhaps one of the most important distinctions between the minding of two-year-olds and of most adults is that two-year-olds have not yet mastered the trick of thinking 'about' things, thinking in concepts rather than in a context. For this they will need a few more years of practice in using language and in noticing how it is used by others.

Language has a special function as a mediating tool which allows public meanings to be negotiated and shared while also allowing private meanings to be revealed in the 'telling' ways in which meanings are performed and expressed differently by different people. When children begin to 'use words' it is easy to imagine that they have already crossed the threshold of language but there is still a long way to go before they are able to join us in our use of public, dictionary-definable, conceptual and decontextualised meanings.

The chapter will conclude with a consideration of how we might understand the role of practitioners whose professional task is to furnish children with the opportunities and experiences which will enable them to enter into a minding community. How can we help two-year-olds and even younger children to manage the transition from context-dependent minding, with the support of familiar people, places, things and routines, to the much more demanding task of minding, making sense and forming relationships among strangers in a strange, new setting?

Intersubjectivity: attention to attention and learning how to mind

> jointness comes with being moved just enough to sense the psychological orientation of the other in oneself, but as the other's. This happens through intersubjective engagement that is emotional in source and emotional in quality.
>
> (Hobson, 2005: 201)

Babies are not born with an inbuilt ability to share attention but they are born into communities which actively support their development of this ability. To understand how children are helped into particular ways of minding, it may be helpful to clarify what is meant by attention and also how attention can be shared.

Peter Hobson (2005: 187) describes attention as 'psychological engagement' and I think it is helpful to move away from the idea of attention as an internal psychological property of an individual, to see it more as a relational concept, a connection between people or between people and things. The development of these connections has been extensively studied by Colwyn Trevarthen and his colleagues, resulting in a clear account of consistent patterns in how babies are helped to develop intersubjective relationships (Trevarthen and Aitken, 2001; Trevarthen, 2011). Beginning with the purely social interpersonal 'conversations' which frame primary intersubjectivity (Trevarthen, 1979) – whether in face-to-face 'chatting' or skin-to-skin connectedness – babies are brought into engagement with encultured adults in a two-way process of mutual familiarisation. Babies appear to enjoy participating in interactions with a partner who pays close attention to them (Parker-Rees, 2007) and Ed Tronick and colleagues (Cohn and Tronick, 1983; see also Adamson and Frick, 2003) showed how sensitive they can be to interruptions in this flow of mutual engagement. If the caregiver switches to 'still face', not responding to the baby's cues, or even if an artificial delay is introduced between action and response, when baby and caregiver are linked remotely via cameras and monitors (Murray and Trevarthen, 1986), babies will quickly start to show signs of unease, first by actively trying to provoke a contingent response, e.g. by waving arms, vocalising and making eye-contact, and then writhing and crying to signal their distress. Even very young babies are clearly sensitive to differences between attuned, intersubjective minding and less attentive forms of interaction.

Trevarthen noted that babies who are able to sit up, making their hands available for exploration of their environment, may switch the focus of their attention to objects they can pick up and manipulate. This 'epoch of games' (Trevarthen,

12 Rod Parker-Rees

1977) can be seen not so much as an interruption in the development of inter-subjectivity as a shift of focus to relationships with things, allowing babies to tune up their understanding of the affordances of different objects without the direct mediation of another person's responses. Handling things allows the baby to explore her relationships with what different objects allow and enable her to do. Reddy (2008) has shown that this apparent shift from a highly social, 'second-person' perspective, to a more 'Piagetian', 'third-person' perspective on what can be done with things is preceded by heightened interest in other people's hands and in their manipulation of objects. So what looks like a very private form of exploration may well be motivated, at least in part, by an early awareness of other people's relationships with things. It is important to recognise that most of the objects encountered and handled by a baby will have been *selected* as 'safe' and 'appropriate' by adults or older children who are versed in a particular culture. So even when a baby is 'alone' with objects to play with, she is still wrapped in the mindings of her community.

Towards the end of the first year, the infant's experience of primary intersub-jectivity and of 'first-hand' exploration of objects enables her to notice another form of relationship in her social environment. Where primary intersubjectivity is focused on the experience of mutually responsive interaction with another person, secondary intersubjectivity (Trevarthen and Hubley, 1978) involves attention to the relationship between another person and a *topic* with which that person is engaging; for example, different adults may respond to a spider with interest, fear or disgust. Familiarity with persons and with objects allows the infant to focus on differences between people's responses to particular objects, events or other people. This is another important step in the continuing development of the infant's ability to communicate and opens up opportunities for participation in the negotiation of shared ways of minding. By focusing attention on what other people are interested in, how they respond to things and what they do with things, the infant can now discover what things *mean* to particular people.

At this point, meanings are not understood as properties of objects ('spiders are interesting/scary/disgusting') but as features of relationships between persons and things, events or other people ('Dad is scared of spiders'). This growing awareness of structure in the patterning of interactions already relies on an ability to generalise across different events, to notice consistencies and repetitions which inform expec-tations and allow the infant to predict how familiar people are likely to respond in familiar situations ('Dad *is* scared of spiders' vs. 'Dad *was* scared of the spider' – though of course this understanding is not yet held or expressed in this verbal form!).

Social referencing, the outsourcing of interpretation by paying attention to the way other people respond to things, is widely recognised as a powerful strategy for 'harvesting' cultural information which other people have already learned. There is, however, much more to this process than just the acquisition of knowledge. Sharing attention is, first and foremost, a way of connecting and communicating with the minding of other people and it is important to recognise the affective, social qualities associated with this experience. Hobson (2005: 201) has argued that 'one can only have joint attention if one has the capacity to 'join' another person' but he has also pointed out that this 'joining' is more complicated than it might at first appear. When we talk about infants developing the ability to share in joint attention with others, it is easy to imagine a meeting of previously separate minds but this is an example of the common tendency to project our adult ways of minding into our interpretation of the experience of children. It is easy to forget that our earliest experiences are not clearly differentiated between 'mine' and 'yours'. We begin our lives in the flow of what Vygotsky described as the 'Great We', immersed in interactions, supported and swept along by them and alert to their felt qualities. We enjoy the 'fit' of attuned interaction with a familiar partner and we feel distress when the flow is disturbed but we do not yet understand our interactions in terms of exchanges between a clearly distinct 'you' and 'me': 'at times interacting caregiver-infant dyads are neither one individual nor two, but somewhere in between' (Spurrett and Cowley, 2010: 308).

I have argued (Parker-Rees, 2014) that recognising differences between other people's ways of responding to objects and events enables infants to construct assemblies of attitudes and behaviours which can be associated with particular persons who have distinct ways of minding. Infants do not need to construct a theory of mind before they can understand that different people demonstrate different kinds of attention to things, but once they are aware of other people's attention they can begin to recognise *themselves* as objects of this attention. Joint attention may not be so much about bringing 'our' attention into line with someone else's as about learning to separate ourself and others *out* of the flow of interaction between us.

There is an important distinction between undifferentiated attention and shared attention, which requires awareness of both joint experience and a distinct, experiencing self. Carpenter and Liebal (2011) offer a powerful account of the pleasure shown by two-year-olds when they register that they are sharing attention, as when a child notices that someone else is imitating her actions. The smile which often accompanies this 'sharing look', after a child has successfully 'locked on' to another person's attention, is evidence of the pleasure which we associate with the sharing of experience, and this pleasure is itself evidence of the value and importance of shared minding.

For most people, sharing attention is a powerful motivator, whether in 'gossip' about social matters or publication of academic arguments and findings. Developments in social media have highlighted our preoccupation both with sharing our experience and with getting feedback ('likes') from others, not least because this sharing allows individuals to function as parts of a sociocultural 'superorganism', both contributing to and fed by information and understanding which extends far beyond our own first-hand experience. Our first steps into a 'shared life' (Heal, 2005: 40) mark the beginnings of our participation in interactions which will both open up a world of other people's experiences and enable us to find ourselves reflected in the eyes and mindings of others.

Internalising and externalising

> Human agency is realised through participation in practices that are 'ours' before they can be 'mine'.
>
> (Rouse, 2007: 514)

Sharing in the minding of others involves both internalising, taking on board awareness of how others can be expected to act and react, and externalising, 'performing' one's own interests and intentions. Participation in the shared life of familiar others ensures that infants are exposed to the patterns in people's behaviour, not only what they do but also, to varying degrees, what they like and dislike, what they value and what they fear. As infants become increasingly adept at interpreting the intentions and feelings behind people's actions, they are able to use this awareness to find out more about how *they* are perceived and *who* they are.

It is easy to think of babies as passive receivers of information, overlooking the extent to which our minding is enabled and constrained by our motor capabilities. Our ability to notice other people's attention and intentions is, however, always informed by what we ourselves are able to *do*. We have seen how the motor skills required for manipulation of objects allow the four- to six-month-old infant to focus her attention on exploring the properties of things, motivated in part by her interest in what other people do with their hands. Esther Thelen, Linda Smith and colleagues (Smith et al., 1999) have shown that older infants who are already able to move autonomously (usually by crawling) are significantly more likely to 'understand' the significance of a change of place in the 'A not B' task. This task involves showing the infant an object at location A, covering it and encouraging the infant to 'find' it. When the child is adept at uncovering the object at location A it is then moved, in full sight, to a different location (location B) and again covered. While young infants will typically continue to search for the object at location A, those who are already independently mobile, and who therefore have personal experience of dealing with changes in their geographical relationships with their environment, are more likely to switch their attention to location B. Children who are not yet independently mobile can also be helped to 'succeed' in this task simply by changing their position (height) between the location A and location B trials.

Campos et al. (2000) have studied links between independent mobility towards the end of the first year and a range of social and cognitive changes including joint attention, fear of heights, distance and size perception and separation anxiety, as well as performance on the 'A not B' task. Of particular interest here is their conclusion that the ability to move away from a caregiver is associated with increased checking of the caregiver's position and focus of attention. As noted in the previous section, it is only when the infant is aware of a separation between her own attention and that of her caregiver that she can recognise and appreciate the *sharing* of attention.

As infants grapple with developing motor skills, they have frequent opportunities to notice differences between what they *want* to do and what they are

The minding of two-year-olds   **15**

able to do, helping them to lay the foundations for an understanding of *intention*. Carpenter and Liebal (2011) describe studies by Liszkowski and colleagues, who examined attempts by 12-month-old infants to share attention by pointing at objects and vocalising. By observing infants' responses when an adult responded to a pointing gesture either by focusing only on the child or only on the object pointed at, the researchers found that infants were clearly not 'satisfied' by these unnatural responses. They would repeat their pointing gesture and became less likely to point in future trials. These infants were willing to work to repair their messages to achieve the result they wanted, which was shared attention to a specific target, and this experience of persevering to achieve a social goal may help infants to notice the intentions behind the actions of other people. When Andrew Meltzoff (1995) showed 18-month-old infants a demonstration of a person manipulating objects (e.g. 'trying' to pull the ends off a dumb-bell) he found that most infants, when given the object, would not simply imitate the adult's actions but would 'complete' them, suggesting that they had inferred an intention in the adult's actions.

Children are not left to find out about the social world of attention and intentions on their own. To varying degrees in different cultures, parents and caregivers actively participate in children's minding, responding with interest to bids for shared attention, providing a 'running commentary', helping children to achieve their goals and/or distracting them from undesirable intentions. Nelson (2007: 102) has described this shared minding as 'parental externalisation of intent' and this unusually explicit co-construction of meaning clearly supports children's entry into the particular values and priorities of the caregiver's culture.

Children are also increasingly able to externalise their own interests and attention, contributing to social interactions with others. As they begin to imitate actions, for example, their versions show exactly which aspects have caught their attention, providing subtle cues which can be picked up by attentive caregivers and which inform the familiarity which enables caregiver and child to understand each other. Bruner (1996: 23) noted the special function of externalisation in making aspects of our knowing 'accessible' to appraisal and interest, not only to others but also to ourselves:

> Externalisation produces a *record* of our mental efforts. One that is 'outside us' rather than vaguely 'in memory.' It is somewhat like producing a draft, a rough sketch, a 'mock-up.' … 'It' relieves us in some measure from the always difficult task of 'thinking about our own thoughts' while often accomplishing the same end. 'It' embodies our thoughts in a form more accessible to reflective efforts. The process of thought and its product become interwoven.
>
> (Bruner, 1996: 23)

Vygotsky (1978: 201) described early pretend play as 'memory in action' and we can understand this not only as physical re-enactment of features which have caught

16 Rod Parker-Rees

a child's attention but also as the processing of these features, externalising them so that the child can make personal sense of them, allowing a personal understanding to be internalised. As a child plays with a particular way of acting, observing her own performance and noticing what she notices, she is also contributing to her developing awareness of herself.

For a two-year-old, living and minding in the small private world of personal experience, the boundary between 'in here' and 'out there' is far from clear-cut. Judy Dunn's study of the lives of two-year olds in their homes (Dunn, 1988) provided powerful evidence of the extent to which these very young children were enabled by their familiarity with the patterns of interaction in which they had grown up. Among members of their family, these children showed that they could participate in a wide range of social activities, including teasing, arguing, telling jokes and making excuses, which, at the time of the study, had not been observed in 'laboratory' studies of two-year-olds. It would perhaps be an over-simplification, therefore, to say that the children observed by Dunn had 'internalised' knowledge of their home environment. This knowledge depended on their ability to interact directly with people, places and things; it was not yet 'in' them, available to be used (with the same degree of confidence) elsewhere.

In familiar environments young children (and indeed all of us) are supported by 'withness thinking' (Shotter, 2012); our minding is extended across people, places and things which 'remind' us about what we might do. For adults this might include a bookshelf filled with books which remind us of ideas we have read about, but a two-year-old is more likely to draw from the affordances of toys and other objects which carry reminders of what can be *done* with them and, of course, from inter-subjective relationships with other people. Two-year-olds live in, from and into the space around them. They will not be able to join us in standing apart from this space and thinking 'about' it until they have developed much more sophisticated language skills.

Language and access to shared meanings

> It is through the relationship with the other that the I emerges, is constructed and maintained; and likewise it is through the relationship with internal others that refection itself emerges and is constructed and maintained.
>
> (Kennedy, 2006: 147)

It is particularly difficult for adults, who are deeply immersed in a mental world organised largely by language, to comprehend how different the minding of two-year-olds (and even three- and four-year-olds) really is.

Preverbal minding, as a form of 'withness thinking', is framed, supported and guided by the immediate context in which the child finds herself; whereas verbal, conceptual minding opens up the possibility of 'aboutness thinking', allowing us to stand back and apart from our physical environment and to venture into alternative worlds, remembering past events, planning or anticipating future ones and exploring possible and imagined contexts. Language allows us to share access to concepts which carry generalised meanings – not the personal, particular meanings first noticed by children in the behaviours and responses of individuals but public, common meanings which are co-constructed in the continuing negotiation and exchange of verbal interactions. Concepts are abstractions, literally 'pulled out' from particular contexts and freed from the tangle of messy details which complicate each person's unique, individual experience. Concepts allow different people to share attention to *kinds* of things without requiring that everyone has previous experience of precisely the same contexts. Most importantly, concepts are constantly renegotiated and recalibrated as people share their interest in what others can be expected to know, feel and care about.

But this extensive web of conceptual knowledge is not acquired or internalised suddenly, as soon as children begin to produce and respond to words. Two-year-olds, who have usually just begun to use a few words, still rely on a concrete, present context to support and enable their minding. They are still some years away from developing the ability to 'lift off' or step out from their immediate context into the more public space of conceptual thinking, but their social environment is usually richly organised in ways which will help them to participate in conversations with other people.

Participating in a social environment enables children to develop familiarity with what can be expected to happen in particular places, at particular times and with particular people. Engagement in mealtimes, dressing and undressing, bathtimes, bedtimes, going to the shops, etc., exposes children to patterns in these daily routines, allowing them to develop expectations about what is likely to happen next. Although every mealtime will be slightly different, there are likely to be common elements which are repeated with enough consistency to allow them to become part of a familiar 'script'. Because parents and other caregivers are themselves participants in wider social and linguistic communities, these scripts, while slightly different in every family, are likely to resemble those of other families which share a similar culture. The shared mindings of cultural groups are built into the language and practices of individuals through their conversations with family members and other people, online forums, books, TV programmes and a wide variety of other media. This means that, within a particular cultural group, the unique, private contexts experienced by individual children are still likely to have much in common with the contexts experienced in other families.

Patterns and routines in everyday life, shaped by the wider framing of cultural norms, enable children to begin to differentiate between what *feels* familiar and what is interestingly (or alarmingly) novel, well before they are able to recall specific memories about previous occasions. Children may delight in playful variations in the details of particular scripts, variations which help to confirm a shared understanding of what is 'normal' and what is 'silly'. Katherine Nelson (2007) has noted that by the age of three, children appear to be able to differentiate between 'script' knowledge (about what *usually* happens) and accounts of a specific event. Nelson argues that, for young children, what we call the 'present' tense is actually

18 Rod Parker-Rees

used to signify the normal features of script knowledge ('I get out of bed, I get dressed and I have my breakfast' or 'Dad is afraid of spiders') while the past tense is used when referring to specific events ('I fell out of my bed' or 'Dad was scared of the spider'). This suggests that distinctions between what usually happens and novel, interesting or remarkable events may be particularly salient for young children who are just beginning to 'work out' the regularities and patterns in what happens around them.

Because adults are embedded in linguistic, conceptual ways of minding, they tend to engage with children 'as if' they were already members of the language users club. This assumption is reinforced when they begin to produce sounds which can be taken for words. When adults chat with children or offer a 'running commentary' on the child's actions, attention and intentions, they help to develop associations between particular contexts and particular sounds but they also provide cultural information about what *they* think is *worth* saying. When familiar adults condense aspects of a child's experience into a verbal narrative, the sifting out of what is 'remarkable' from what 'goes without saying' provides valuable information, not only about shared, common understandings of what can be expected but also about the unique features of different people's 'ways of seeing'. When older children struggle to respond to the familiar question, 'what did you do at nursery/school today?' their difficulty may be more to do with deciding *what* will be interesting than with knowing *how* to express themselves.

Nelson (2007) notes that advances in language, like earlier advances in mobility, may result in a need for new strategies to monitor relationships with other people. Two-year-olds are usually still firmly rooted in contextual minding and largely unable to engage in conversations about other times and places, so they do not *need* to notice differences between 'what happened to me' and 'what someone told me about'. As they develop more sophisticated language skills, however, allowing them to stray further away from the here-and-now, it will become increasingly necessary for them to keep track of this distinction between their 'own' experience and 'hearsay' – information about other people's experience. The development of an 'autobiographical self' is driven by this need to differentiate between what is privately 'mine' or 'yours' and what is publicly 'ours'.

Implications for the minding of two-year-olds

> Children's intellect develops through their encounters with the socially mediated world of people doing things in places.
>
> (Engel, 2005: 71)

Other chapters in this volume will elaborate on the details of what two-year-olds need from their caregivers, whether at home or in an early years setting. Here I can only touch on the possible implications of a shift towards seeing children's minding as a shared, social process.

The growing focus on naturalistic observation of very young children in social situations, particularly by female researchers (Dunn, 1988; Rogoff, 2003; Engel, 2005; Nelson, 2007; Reddy, 2008), has helped to highlight the context-dependent, situated nature of early forms of thinking, focusing, noticing and remembering. Instead of trying to devise artificial ways of identifying patterns of development in what individual children are able to do without the support of a familiar context, these researchers have examined the ways in which the ordinary, day-to-day life of communities performs the important pedagogical function of helping children to join in and enjoy the experience of sharing meanings.

Political pressure to get mothers 'back to work' has perhaps contributed to concerns that children are being hurried into care settings which struggle to provide the familiar, intimate kinds of support which children need. The emphasis, in out-of-home settings, on ensuring that every child has a consistent key worker, can be seen as a way of trying to smooth the transition from the familiar context of home to the new, strange and bustling environment of an early years setting but it is important to recognise that these settings can offer rich and exciting opportunities for children to 'move on' from the security and familiarity of 'home' to the novelty and stimulation of 'away'.

While it is certainly possible for children to move on from context-dependent 'withness thinking' to more conceptual, linguistic 'aboutness thinking' within the small world of their immediate family, encounters with a wider variety of different perspectives can contribute to development of broader, more flexible concepts. Like the nurseries of Reggio Emilia, we perhaps need to focus more on supporting communities of children and adults which allow minding to be shared. Instead of worrying about how an early years practitioner can provide fully attuned attention to each child, we should perhaps consider how practitioners can work to maintain and develop a community in which attention is more distributed. Ideally, perhaps, this community would include parents, grandparents, caregivers and other family members so that children have opportunities to participate in a wide range of different kinds of interactions, not only with other two-year-olds, and so that parents and others can also experience the pleasure of joining in with a community beyond the home.

In the past it would have been easy to argue that two-year-olds are not 'ready' to participate in communities outside their family and the assumption that they are developmentally unable to form worthwhile peer relationships could find support in group situations where children were encouraged to explore their own interests. However, when children are expected and helped to take an interest in each other's interests, as well as in those of familiar adults, they can surprise us with their ability to share their minding.

In her deceptively simple account of the relationships between Mrs Tully and the two-year-olds in her classroom, Vivien Gussin Paley (2001) provides a powerful image of how a sensitive adult can support the minding of two-year-olds, helping them to broaden each other's horizons as they get to know each other. Mrs Tully uses Paley's approach to 'doing stories' (Paley, 1981), which involves writing down the children's stories and then, later in the morning, encouraging the children to perform them for each other. Paley describes the children's engagement with Alex's one-word story, 'Mama'. After watching Alex's performance, all of the other children eagerly take turns at presenting their own interpretation of 'Mama':

> Each acts the role according to some inner logic: this one walks on his toes, another bends to touch the rug, someone else closes her eyes and sways. … Their ability to bring a character to life and reveal something about themselves at the same time is astonishing'.
>
> (Paley, 2001: 4–5)

As each child externalises and shares a personal response, the whole group, including Mrs Tully and the performer, is able to share and internalise new meanings. Noticing how other children notice different aspects of the idea of 'Mama' does two important things: it expands what may previously have been a very private association between word and sense into something more like a shared concept and, at the same time, it allows each child (and Mrs Tully) to get to know more about the distinctiveness of each child's unique perspective.

Paley notes that the sign on Mrs Tully's door reads 'Lillian Tully, director and head teacher' but I think this account of her ability to draw children into a community of shared meanings shows that she was also a highly skilled childminder.

Questions

> When you spend time with two-year-olds, what do you do that might help them to join you in your social world?
>
> Is it possible to establish a clear boundary between 'your' minding and the children's?

Recommended reading

Nelson, K. (2007). *Young Minds in Social Worlds: experience, meaning and memory*. Cambridge, MA: Harvard University Press.

Katherine Nelson offers an excellent review of research into the distinctive features of young children's thinking. In this book she traces the fascinating, shifting relationships between what children are able to do and what they learn from participating in the everyday interactions which make up their social worlds. Nelson shows how children are minded by interactions with older children and adults who actively help them to join in.

References

Adamson, L. and Frick, J. (2003). The still face: a history of a shared experimental paradigm. *Infancy*, 4(4), 451–473.

Bruner, J. (1996). *The Culture of Education*. Cambridge, MA: Harvard University Press

Campos, J., Anderson, D., Barbu-Roth, M., Hubbard, E., Hertenstein, M. and Witherington, D. (2000). Travel broadens the mind. *Infancy*, 1(2), 149–220.

Carpenter, M. and Liebal, K. (2011). Joint attention, communication and knowing together in infancy. In A. Seeman (ed.), *Joint Attention: new developments in psychology, philosophy of mind, and social neuroscience*. Cambridge, MA: MIT Press, 159–81.

Cohn, J. and Tronick, E. (1983). Three-month-old infants' reaction to simulated maternal depression. *Child Development*, 54(1), 185–193.

Dunn, J. (1988). *The Beginnings of Social Understanding*. Oxford: Blackwell.

Engel, S. (2005). *Real Kids: creating meaning in everyday life*. Cambridge, MA: Harvard University Press.

Heal, J. (2005). Joint attention and understanding the mind. In N. Eilan, C. Hoerl, T. McCormack and J. Roessler (eds.), *Joint Attention: communication and other minds*. Oxford: Oxford University Press, 34–44.

Hobson, P. (2005). What puts the jointness into joint attention. In N. Eilan, C. Hoerl, T. McCormack and J. Roessler (eds.), *Joint Attention: communication and other minds*. Oxford: Oxford University Press, 185–204.

Kennedy, D. (2006). *The Well of Being: childhood, subjectivity and education*. Albany, NY: State University of New York Press.

Meltzoff, A. (1995). Understanding the intentions of others: re-enactment of intended acts by 18-month-old children. *Developmental Psychology*, 31(5), 838–850.

Murray, L. and Trevarthen, C. (1986). The infant's role in mother–infant communications. *Journal of Child Language*, 13(1), 15–29.

Nelson, K. (2007). *Young Minds in Social Worlds: experience, meaning and memory*. Cambridge, MA: Harvard University Press.

Paley, V. G. (1981). *Wally's Stories: conversations in the kindergarten*. Cambridge, MA: Harvard University Press.

Paley, V. G. (2001). *In Mrs Tully's Room*. Cambridge, MA: Harvard University Press.

Parker-Rees, R. (2007). Liking to be liked: imitation, familiarity and pedagogy in the first years of life. *Early Years*, 27(1), 3–17.

Parker-Rees, R. (2014). Playfulness and the co-construction of identity in the first years. In L. Brooker, S. Edwards and M. Blaise (eds.), *The SAGE Handbook of Play and Learning in Early Childhood*. London: Sage, 366–77.

Reddy, V. (2008). *How Infants Know Minds*. Cambridge, MA: Harvard University Press.

Rogoff, B. (2003). *The Cultural Nature of Human Development*. Oxford: Oxford University Press.

Rouse, J. (2007). Practice Theory. *Division 1 Faculty Publications*. Paper 43. Available at: http://wesscholar.wesleyan.edu/div1facpubs/43 499–540 (Accessed on: 08/08/2017)

Shotter, J. (2012). More than cool reason: 'withness-thinking' or 'systemic thinking' and 'thinking *about* systems'. *International Journal of Collaborative Practices*, 3(1), 1–13.

Smith, L., Thelen, E., Titzer, R. and McLin, D. (1999). Knowing in the context of acting: the task dynamics of the A not B error. *Psychological Review*, 106(2), 235–260.

Spurrett, D. and Cowley, S. (2010). The extended infant: utterance activity and distributed cognition. In R. Menary (ed.), *The Extended Mind*. Cambridge, MA: MIT Press, 295–324.

Trevarthen, C. (1977). Descriptive analyses of infant communication behaviour. In H.R. Schaffer (ed.), *Studies in Mother-infant Interaction: Proceedings of the Loch Lomond Symposium, Ross Priory, University of Strathclyde, September, 1975*. London: Academic Press.

Trevarthen, C. (1979). Communication and cooperation in early infancy: a description of primary intersubjectivity. In M. Bullowa (ed.), *Before Speech: the beginning of interpersonal communication*. Cambridge: Cambridge University Press, 321–347.

Trevarthen, C. (2011). The generation of human meaning: how shared experience grows in infancy. In A. Seeman (ed.), *Joint Attention: new developments in psychology, philosophy of mind, and social neuroscience*. Cambridge, MA: MIT Press, 73–113.

Trevarthen, C. and Aitken, K. (2001). Infant intersubjectivity: research, theory and clinical applications. *Journal of Child Psychology and Psychiatry*, 42(1), 3–48.

Trevarthen, C. and Hubley, P. (1978). Secondary intersubjectivity: confidence, confiding and acts of meaning in the first year. In A. Lock (ed.), *Action, Gesture and Symbol: the emergence of language*. London: Academic Press, 183–229.

Vygotsky, L. S. (1978). *Mind in Society: the development of higher psychological processes*. Cambridge, MA: Harvard University Press.

Vygotsky, L. S. (1998). *The Collected Works of L. S. Vygotsky. Vol 5: Child Psychology*. New York: Springer.

3

VULNERABLE IDENTITIES

Anita Soni

Introduction

This chapter begins with an examination of critical and sensitive periods of development, and how this relates to the current policy of providing funded nursery places for disadvantaged two-year-olds. This is followed by a section on identity development in two-year-olds, a theme which will be considered further in Chapter 5; here, the focus is on how terms such as 'disadvantaged' may impact upon the children themselves, their families and their engagement with targeted funding. The chapter goes on to consider vulnerability and related concepts of resilience, risk and protective factors, the evidence base for these concepts and in turn their implications for practice. Vulnerability is concerned with predisposition or susceptibility to delayed or disordered development following adversity, while resilience generally refers to positive adaptation in the face of adversity. Although some children face stressful, high-risk situations during their early years of life, they nonetheless go on to succeed in life, and this appears to be related to the balance between risk factors and protective factors in their individual contexts. The chapter will reflect on how practitioners' support for children in funded nursery places for two-year-olds might decrease risk factors and promote protective factors, thereby helping children to overcome their initial disadvantage and ultimately prevent social exclusion.

Critical or sensitive periods of development?

In considering the development of young children, it is important to examine key ideas around critical and sensitive periods of development. Schaffer (1996) cites Lorenz (1935) as formalising thinking that early experiences are irreversible and are therefore 'critical'. This implies that the learning that results from these experiences is absolute and unchangeable. Lorenz's ideas of critical early experiences were based on his observations of the imprinting phenomenon. This referred to certain species of bird forming an attachment to the parent within a critical period of time after birth. If instead the bird was exposed to another species, the bird could attach to that species or, if not exposed at all during this time, it did not then develop any attachments and remained socially isolated.

However, this concept of the critical period with irreversible outcomes has subsequently been challenged and replaced with the term 'sensitive period', whereby the probability of certain forms of learning are increased and other times decreased, rather than being positioned as impossible (Schaffer, 1996). Knudsen (2004) illustrated this difference effectively through examples of critical and sensitive periods in mammals and birds. He identified binocular vision in mammals as developing within a critical period. During this critical period, Knudsen (2004) cites Antonini and Stryker (1993), who stated that if one eyelid of the mammal is closed, this causes a selective elimination of connections from the closed eye and an elaboration of new connections from the open eye. Typical binocular vision cannot be regained or recovered even if visual input is restored to both eyes at a later point in time. In comparison, Knudsen (2004) identified auditory processing of spatial information in barn owls as an example of a sensitive period, as there is a high degree of plasticity in barn owl development. In barn owls, the typical representations of auditory cue values can be acquired even after the juvenile period ends, by restoring normal vision and hearing and access to a sufficiently rich environment.

Initially, Bowlby (1951) believed there was a critical period for attachment in humans, and that beyond this time period it was impossible to achieve a secure attachment. He identified the critical period as being between birth and two-and-a-half years. However, research on adopted children who lived in institutions for the early part of their lives by Tizard (1977) and Hodges and Tizard (1989) contradicted this. The research indicated that the majority of the adopted children did develop relationships with their adopted family even when the adoption occurred beyond the identified threshold age of two-and-a-half years. However, regarding social relationships with others, there were further difficulties such as the children having fewer friends and being over-affectionate with strangers. Schaffer (1996) states that this evidence contradicts the idea of a critical period for children to develop emotional attachments, and suggests instead that there is a sensitive period for social development.

More recently, Rutter's work within the English and Romanian Adoptees (ERA) study (Rutter et al., 2009) compared the development of children at 6, 11 and 15 years. The study compared the outcomes of children who experienced institutional care in Romania until at least the age of six months with a group of children adopted within the UK who did not experience institutional care and a control group of children. Rutter et al. (2009) identified that the children from the Romanian orphanages showed severe impairment in their average development level, but went on to make remarkable gains psychologically and physically after being adopted.

Rutter et al. (2009) identified that the most important predictive factor of later psychological problems was the age of the child when leaving institutional care to join the adoptive family. He identified that there were negligible psychological problems in children who left institutional care at a younger age, such as six months. Nelson et al. (2007) suggest there is a possible sensitive period of the first two years of life for cognitive development. The findings indicate that the younger the child is when placed in foster care, the better the outcome, and the longer the child remains in institutional care, the greater the cost. However, as both Nelson et al. (2007) and Rutter et al. (2009) point out, it is difficult to identify the parameters of the sensitive period definitively. Rutter et al. (2009) instead highlight the significance of a lack of crucially important experiences with respect to social interaction, play and conversation, thereby highlighting the key role of the environment.

Implications for policy and practice

Research on critical and sensitive periods has a key role to play in considering the provision of funded nursery places for disadvantaged two-year-olds. Evidence on the development of attachments indicates that early intervention is important for the social and emotional well-being of children who might, for various reasons, be missing out on opportunities for social interaction. The evidence suggests that there may be benefits in targeting funding for two-year-olds as some may be disadvantaged in this way and this age has been found to be a sensitive period for both social and cognitive development. However, in the context of the funded place for two-year-olds policy, it is vital to reflect on what the research has shown about the sensitivity of this period of development and what is needed to support child development. Rutter et al. (2009) and Nelson et al. (2007) highlight the need for children to gain opportunities to interact socially, to play and talk to others, both adults and children. The Wave Trust/DfE (2013) also highlights the importance of good-quality relationships and secure attachment for young children aged birth to two years. These factors promote the young child's social development, which in turn provides the foundations for developing self-control. For many young children, this takes place in the context of relationships with their parents or carers, siblings and wider family; for some children, particularly with the advent of the two-year-olds funding, this will include the relationships formed with staff and other children in the early years setting.

The Department for Education (DfE, 2014a) identified that 288,930 (42%) of two-year-olds were accessing funded and non-funded early education places. However, Ofsted (2015) note that around 113,000 two-year-olds who were eligible for 15 hours of free early education did not take up their place, representing 42% of all eligible children. Therefore, there are two groups of children to consider – those whose parents elect for them to take up the additional funding to access a place in an early years setting, and those who do not. It is equally important to have services to support both of the groups of children and their families, those who access two-year-old funded early education places and those who do not (see Chapter 8 for

26 Anita Soni

comments on the extent to which the two-year-olds funding initiative offered such opportunities). For the 58% of two-year-olds who are in early years settings, the practitioners working with them need to have a good understanding of early child development, a finding echoed by stakeholders when asked about important factors contributing to high-quality provision for funded two-year-olds (see Chapter 4 for fuller discussion of the relationship between quality and knowledge of child development).

In particular, the Wave Trust/DfE (2013) advocates that practitioners working with children aged from birth to three years have an understanding of young children's social and emotional development, their behaviour and what this communicates, and have realistic expectations of their development. It highlights that practitioners need to understand how attachments develop, and how cultural, social and emotional factors may contribute to behavioural problems in children. It also advocates practitioners being skilled in developing warm relationships with the children they work with. This is enshrined in the Key Person approach (a named member of staff with responsibilities for a small group of children to help each child feel safe and cared for) in the Statutory Guidance for the Early Years Foundation Stage (DfE, 2014b), but the guidance on how to develop practice in this area is limited.

Identity

Understanding identity in the early years often begins with considering the work of James (1890, 1892) who distinguishes between two aspects of self: the subjective self (I) and the objective self (me). The objective self, which has become to be known as self-concept, is the collection of beliefs a person holds about themselves, although this is closely entwined with the subjective self (the 'distinct, experiencing self' of Chapter 2) as this creates the self-concept. Bee (2000) makes this clearest by explaining that when you answer 'Who am I?', it is the objective self (me) that you are describing, but it is the 'I' who is doing the describing.

According to developmental psychology, the subjective self is said to develop in the first year, as the child begins to see him/herself as an agent in the world who can make things happen. The second major step highlighted by Bee (2000) is that the child comes to understand that she or he is an object in the world, and develops an understanding of the objective self (me). This self-awareness has been measured in a number of ways, with the most famous being through the use of mirrors and use of name when seeing a picture of themselves. Lewis and Brooks-Gunn (1978) found that no child aged 9–12 months identified themselves in the mirror but by 21 months, three-quarters recognised themselves. It is important to recognise that a range of factors play a role in when a child develops self-recognition, including infant attachment (Lewis and Shaefer, 1985) and parenting style (Keller et al., 2004) amongst other social factors.

Lewis (1990) proposed that once children have self-awareness and understand they have agency, the categorical self appears. This is when children, through their social interaction with others, begin to understand the different categories they belong to. Sameroff's (1991) transactional model of development emphasises the reciprocal interaction between the child, the parents and the environment in relation to the child's personal, social and emotional development. The sociocultural context is important in shaping the categorical self. Rochat (2010) argues that, by two years, a child has an understanding of themselves as a separate individual and that their physical self is evaluated by others. Rochat (2010) bases this on the research by Lewis (1999) on toddlers' identification of themselves in mirrors showing embarrassment, by hiding their face or avoiding the reflection, or by acting out in a self-conscious way. This highlights that two-year-olds not only have a sense of self but can feel self-conscious emotions such as embarrassment, shame, pride and contempt (Lewis, 1995, 1999), and has implications for targeted support for children and families.

Implications for policy and practice

As a child has an understanding of him or herself by the age of two as described above, there may be difficulties with targeted support such as funded places for two-year-olds. The child as an individual may not at two years be aware of being the target of support; this develops over time. The child's family will be aware and may not identify with the label of 'disadvantage'. This highlights the importance of practitioners understanding how children's identity develops, and their role in developing children's positive sense of self. The Wave Trust/DfE (2013) highlight the importance of taking a universal approach to the promotion of positive mental health in young children, and see this as interwoven with the mental health of parents and caregivers. This has implications for who should be targeted for additional funding, how the provision is understood as for children *and their families*, not the child alone, and how this funding is labelled and described to enable positive uptake by families.

There are also difficulties associated with what is categorised as disadvantage. The criteria for eligibility for two-year funding have changed as, over time, the criteria for identification of disadvantage have changed. In the pilot study, where over 13,500 children were provided with free early years education between 2006 and 2008, Local Authorities (LAs) could select their own criteria for offering places as long as the child was not accessing any formal childcare. Kazimirski et al. (2008) identified that some LAs gave a universal offer in particular wards where deprivation was at a high level, alongside targeted approaches that tended to focus on disadvantage related to the following three areas:

- **Disadvantage relating to broad family group or circumstances**: Black and Minority Ethnic (BME) families, families with English as an additional language (EAL), traveller/Gypsy/Romany families, refugee/asylum-seeking families, families living in a hostel or temporary accommodation, families on low income/benefits, workless households.

28 Anita Soni

- **Disadvantage relating to specific needs of parent**: teenage parents, experience of domestic violence, significant caring responsibilities, substance misusers and lone parents.
- **Disadvantage relating to specific needs of child**: being looked after, on Child Protection Register (CPR), child with additional needs (for example, statemented), physical disabilities, learning difficulties, behavioural difficulties, language or communication difficulties.

Smith et al. (2009) identify that the vast majority of children within the pilot study were 'disadvantaged', with 73% living in the 20% most disadvantaged areas of the country. This included lone parents and there was a higher prevalence of longstanding illnesses and disabilities amongst both parents and children involved in the pilot study. More children involved in the pilot study were identified as having additional needs than in the general population (most commonly with difficulties with speech and language). Smith et al. (2009) emphasised the variation in size between the LAs taking part in the pilot study, and therefore the number of places available also varied (ranging from 20 to 750 places per school term). LAs tended to base their estimates of the number of places on either demand from parents and/or capacity within the childcare sector.

The two-year-olds funding offer was extended in 2009 (Gibb et al., 2011), and shifted towards a focus on economically disadvantaged families. This then became the foremost factor in deciding eligibility, and took the focus away from other types of disadvantage such as parents' own difficulties and other vulnerability issues. The eligibility criteria were tightly focused on economic deprivation, using the proxy measure of eligibility for free school meals, rather than considering family circumstances, parent needs or the specific needs of children.

In more recent years, the Department for Education has allowed LAs to recognise other forms of disadvantage within children themselves, such as being looked after by the LA; subject to a special guardianship order, child arrangement order or adoption order; having a special educational need or disability as demonstrated by a statement of special educational needs, an education, health and care (EHC) plan or claiming for Disability Living Allowance. LAs continue to have some minimal flexibility in who the funding will target and to have additional criteria, such as whether the child is on a Child Protection or Child in Need Plan, is subject to a Common Assessment Framework (CAF) or has significant special educational needs as identified by a professional. However, the eligibility criteria for being a disadvantaged two-year-old focuses on either family economic disadvantage or within-child factors, rather than considering the broader environments in which the child spends their time. This would include both the family environment and the community beyond. Therefore, within the current criteria for eligibility, it would be helpful to have recognition of family factors to reach parents experiencing particular difficulties, such as domestic violence, mental health difficulties or special educational needs or disabilities.

Vulnerability and resilience

Schaffer (1996) argues that it is oversimplistic to assume that particular childhood experiences will definitely lead to a specific outcome in adulthood; instead, multiple outcomes are possible. This builds on the earlier challenges to the concept of a critical period. Instead, he highlights the role of risk and protective factors, and how these lead to some children having a greater vulnerability to stress, whereas others may be more resilient. Risk factors are those that would increase the probability of an undesirable outcome as a result of exposure to stress, and protective factors are those that buffer children against negative outcomes. Schaffer (1996) reinforces that vulnerability and resilience are not fixed and can change over time and place, and that these factors do not act in isolation but interact with each other.

Risk and protective factors have been identified through longitudinal research such as that conducted by Werner (1989, 1993) and Werner and Smith (1982). This research collected information on individuals, many of whom faced considerable disadvantage, including poverty, parental substance abuse and family disruption, at ages 2, 10, 18 and 32. The research examined the risk and protective factors that influenced whether children were resilient or vulnerable to the stresses they experienced. One-third of the nearly 700 infants were identified as high-risk, as they encountered four or more cumulative risk factors such as experiencing moderate to severe degrees of perinatal stress, poverty, being raised by mothers with little formal education, or living in a troubled family environment. Of this one-third, 72 were identified as resilient, and Werner (1989) identified a number of characteristics within the individuals, their families and in their wider environment that contributed to their resilience. Werner (1989) stated that both vulnerability and resiliency are not fixed, but are relative, and so can change over time. Masten (2001: 228) states that 'resilience refers to a class of phenomena characterized by *good outcomes in spite of serious threats to adaptation or development*' (italics in original). She identifies that resilience requires two key judgements: that individuals must have faced a significant threat or demonstrable risk to their development, and that there must be positive outcomes.

In Werner's work, at the individual level, gender played a key role, and boys were more vulnerable to negative outcomes in the first decade of their lives in terms of developing perinatal difficulties, developing challenging behaviour, having difficulties at school and acquiring a delinquency record. However, girls became more vulnerable during adolescence. A second significant factor was the child's temperament, with children described as very active, affectionate and good-natured as being resilient, which in turn elicited positive attention from family members and others. The resilient children also had fewer eating and sleep habits that distressed their parents. One aspect of their temperament that was seen at age 20 months was that they were children with a positive social orientation, who were confident to seek new experiences, and were advanced in communication, movement and self-help skills.

30 Anita Soni

Schaffer (1996) identified some factors external to the child that can influence children's susceptibility to stress. These include:

- the level of harmony and conflict within the family;
- the availability of close supportive attachments to a parent;
- parent caregiving style;
- availability of substitute caregivers beyond parents;
- separation of child from parents;
- number of and spacing of children in the family;
- parent's ability to be available to their child (such as not negatively impacted on by mental health or substance abuse); and
- poverty.

In school, Werner (1989) identified that resilient children tended to make best use of the skills they had, were engaged in different interests and activities and had good reasoning and reading skills, although they might not be especially gifted. Family factors included that the family tended to have four or fewer children with spacing of two or more years between siblings, and that the child had the opportunity to develop a strong bond with one caregiver who gave positive attention to the child. This bond did not have to be within the nuclear family, and could come from grandparents, regular babysitters or neighbours. Werner (1989) identified factors beyond the family, including the need for emotional support outside the family through an informal network of extended family, neighbours, peers and other key adults such as neighbours and teachers. At school age, many of the resilient children had several close friends.

Sroufe et al. (2005) in the US longitudinal study, the Minnesota Study of Risk and Adaptation from Birth to Adulthood, followed 180 children born into poverty from birth onwards. The study concluded that resilience in the face of adversity was due to children having 'a positive platform or balancing supports available later' (p. 227) where a 'positive platform' refers to early experiences with carers both at home and beyond. Masten (2001) brings together the research on resilience, and identifies that studies on resilience initially sought to identify extraordinary qualities but that resilience results from 'ordinary human adaptive processes' (p. 234). She identifies these as having attachments to capable, caring adults in the family and community, having cognitive and self-regulation skills, positive self-image, and the motivation to be effective.

Johnston-Wilder and Collins (2008) highlight the importance of fostering resilience rather than seeking to reduce or eliminate risk factors. Indeed, Newman (2004) argues that children and young people need an opportunity to practise and develop their coping strategies in challenging situations. He highlights a number of key strategies for children to help them develop resilience in their pre-school years and infancy including:

- social support for mothers, to moderate perinatal stress;
- parent education;

- safe play areas and provision of learning materials; and
- high-quality pre-school daycare.

Rutter (1987) argued against simply identifying a list of protective factors, and instead looked at the contexts and developmental mechanisms that enabled these factors to protect against psychopathology. Rutter (1987) identified four mediating mechanisms that act as predictors in protective processes: reduction of risk impact; reduction of negative chain reactions; bolstering of self-esteem and self-efficacy; and having opportunities at key turning points in life.

This argument is exemplified by Dweck's study (1999) on children's beliefs about their own abilities, self-efficacy, which found that children either believed their intelligence was fixed and therefore unable to be changed or that their abilities could be improved through work and effort. Dweck (1999) found that the children with growth mindsets, that is, those who thought their abilities could be improved by hard work, had greater resilience in coping as the work or the learning became more difficult, and in turn achieved more.

There are critiques of this approach to understanding vulnerability and resilience. Smith (2015) argues against using the term 'resilience' and suggests using the term coined by Martin and Marsh (2008), 'academic buoyancy'. This is based on the key idea that much of the research on resilience, such as that by Werner and Smith (1982), Werner (1989, 1993), Rutter (1987) and Sroufe et al. (2005), is based on children at risk of psychopathology, and is not based on how individuals cope with minor daily setbacks and smaller-scale adversity. Martin and Marsh (2008) argue that buoyancy differs from resilience in that it is not based on acute extreme adversity but relates instead to everyday setbacks. It is focused on building strengths proactively rather than reactively managing challenges and setbacks. Although this research is based on young people of high school age in Australia, and therefore focuses on factors that relate to the students themselves such as self-efficacy, engagement, control and anxiety, it does also include teacher–student relationships. This has relevance to younger children in terms of their relationships with practitioners, and in particular their Key Person (see below).

Implications for policy and practice

The policy of providing early education for two-year-olds experiencing disadvantage could be said to play a role in the reduction of risk impact. This support for children can be viewed as a buffer or a protective factor for children exposed to the risk factors of poverty, special educational needs or disability, or being looked after by the LA. It could also be viewed as an opportunity to disrupt the cycle of negative chain reactions (Rutter, 1987), as it may give families a respite from looking after young children and reduce opportunities for parent–child conflict when there are other stresses within the family home.

Of particular relevance to practice with young children is Rutter's (1987) focus on the role of self-esteem, people's feelings about themselves, and self-efficacy, people's beliefs in their abilities to deal with life's challenges and to control what happens to them. He identifies the importance of secure and harmonious personal relationships at an early age and, although he locates these in relation to parents, he does make the point that other relationships also play a role. This could be said to include relationships with early years practitioners, and so supports the value of the Key Person approach (Elfer et al., 2011). Elfer et al. describe the Key Person approach as:

> a way of working in nurseries in which the whole focus and organisation is aimed at enabling and supporting close attachments between individual children and individual staff.
>
> (Elfer et al., 2011: 23).

In terms of research on how Key Person relationships can be established, Howes (1999) states that the key determinants as to whether a child forms a bond with non-maternal caregivers (those who provide care but are not the child's mother) include:

* whether the caregiver provides both physical and emotional care;
* whether that person is a consistent presence within the child's social network; and
* whether the caregiver has an emotional investment in the child.

Although this research is based on all those who give care to children, beyond mothers, there are some important messages for practitioners who work with young children. Within early years settings that provide care and education outside the family, there needs to be a consistent early years practitioner who is with the child over a period of time, engages in looking after and caring for the child and emotionally invests in the child.

The second aspect Rutter identifies is the role of successful task accomplishment. Although Rutter's research was located within school, it too has application to early years provision. He identifies that this means that tasks or challenges should be within children's coping strategies, which could be said to support the importance of developmentally appropriate practice for young children. This would imply a stronger focus on child-led activities and a reduction in adult-led or large-group activities for which children have not yet developed appropriate attention and social abilities. In terms of the role of the adult, Roberts (2010) identifies five principles of companionable learning to support children's well-being:

* agency in companionable play – the child is given the idea that they can make a difference to and have some control of their play;
* anchored attention – the child knows that they have guaranteed times where they enjoy the companionable and full attention of their Key Person, and further, that they are kept in the Key Person's mind;

- companionable attention – the child having the full and undivided attention of their Key Person;
- companionable apprenticeship – children taking part in real and purposeful tasks and routines where they can help; and
- a child's personal time and space – going at the pace of the child, allowing them sufficient time to do or think about things.

Conclusion

This chapter has considered the benefit of targeted funding aimed at two-year-old children, and how this fits with research into sensitive periods of development. It argues that it is vital that practitioners working with this age group understand the social and emotional aspects of young children's development, and enable children to develop secure attachments both at home and in the early years provision. It is important to consider not only the needs of the children that access the additional funding and the early years provision, but also the children whose parents choose not to access this provision. The chapter has examined research on vulnerability and resilience, and considered how this relates to disadvantage. Because, in addition to two-year olds who have a recognised special educational need, funding for two-year-olds has been targeted at families who face economic disadvantage, using free school meals as a proxy measure. This means that other forms of disadvantage, particularly those faced by the parents, may not be recognised.

Questions

What can settings do to reduce the influence of the label 'disadvantaged' on a child's developing identity?

How would you respond to a colleague concerned that children might become too dependent on their Key Person?

Further reading

Roberts, R. (2010). *Wellbeing from Birth*, London: Sage Publications.

This book is about the importance of collective well-being in settings. Based on a strong theoretical framework, it includes practical strategies for work with diverse families, but also discusses the well-being of practitioners. This includes developing the Key Person approach, the power of play and making the most of everyday interactions with children and their parents.

References

Antonini, A. and Stryker, M. P. (1993). Rapid remodeling of axonal arbors in the visual cortex, *Science*, 260, 1819–1821

Bee, H. (2000). *The Developing Child* (9th edition), Boston, MA: Allyn and Bacon.

Bowlby, J. (1951). *Maternal Care and Mental Health*, Geneva, Switzerland: World Health Organization.

Department for Education (DfE). (2014a) *Statistical First Release: Provision for children under five years of age in England*, London: DfE.

Department for Education (DfE) (2014b). *Statutory Framework for the Early Years Foundation Stage*, London: DfE.

Dweck, C. S. (1999). *Self-Theories: Their role in motivation, personality and development*, Philadelphia, PA: Taylor and Francis

Elfer, P., Goldschmied, E. and Selleck, D. (2011). *Key Persons in the Nursery: Building relationships for quality provision*, Oxon: David Fulton Publishers.

Gibb, J., Jelicic, H., La Valle, I., Gowland, S., Kinsella, R., Jessiman, P. and Ormston R., (2011). *Rolling Out Free Early Education for Disadvantaged Two-year-olds: An implementation study for local authorities and providers*. Research report DFE-RR131, London: DfE.

Hodges, J. and Tizard, B. (1989). Social and family relationships of ex-institutional adolescents, *Journal of Child Psychology and Psychiatry*, 30, 77–97.

Howes, C. (1999). Attachment relationships in the context of multiple carers. In Cassidy, J. and Shaver, P. R. (eds.), *Handbook of Attachment*. New York: The Guildford Press, 671–687.

James, W. (1890). *Principles of Psychology*, Chicago: Encyclopaedia Britannica.

James, W. (1892). *Psychology: The briefer course*, New York: Holt.

Johnston-Wilder, S. and Collins J. (2008). Children negotiating identities. In Collins, J. and Foley, P. (eds.), *Promoting Children's Wellbeing: Policy and practice*. Milton Keynes: The Open University and Bristol: Policy Press, 41–74.

Kazimirski, A., Dickens, S. and White, C. (2008). *Pilot Scheme for Two Year Old Children: Evaluation of outreach approaches*. DCSF research report no. DCSF-RR021. Nottingham: DCSF Publications.

Keller, H., Yovsi, R., Borke, J., Kartner, J., Jensen, H. and Papligoura, Z. (2004). Developmental consequences of early parenting experiences: Self-recognition and self-regulation in three cultural communities, *Child Development*, 75(6), 1745–1760.

Knudsen, E. I. (2004). Sensitive periods in the development of the brain and behaviour, *Journal of Cognitive Neuroscience*, 16(8), 1412–1425.

Lewis, M. (1990). Social knowledge and social development, *Merrill-Palmer Quarterly*, 36(1), 93–116.

Lewis, M. (1995). Aspects of the self: From systems to ideas. In Rochat, P. (ed) *The Self in Infancy: Theory and research*. Amsterdam: North-Holland, Elsevier Publishers, 95–116.

Lewis, M. (1999). Social cognition and the self. In Rochat, P. (ed) *Early Social Cognition: Understanding others in the first months of life*. Mahwah, NJ: Lawrence Erlbaum Associates, 81–98.

Lewis, M. and Brooks-Gunn, J. (1978). Self-knowledge and emotional development. In Lewis, M. and Rosenblum, L. A. (eds.), *The Development of Affect*. New York: Plenum Press, 205–226.

Lewis, M. and Shaefer, S. (1985). Peer behaviour and mother–child interaction in maltreated children. In Lewis, M. and Rosenblum, L. (eds.), *The Uncommon Child. Genesis of behaviour Volume 3*. New York: Plenum, 193–224.

Lorenz, K. (1935). Der Kumpan in der Umwelt des Vogels. Der Artgenosse als auslösendes Moment sozialer Verhaltensweisen, *Journal für Ornithologie*, 83, 137–215, 289–413.

Martin, A. J and Marsh, H. W. (2008). Academic buoyancy: Towards an understanding of students' everyday academic resilience, *Journal of School Psychology*, 46(1), 53–83.

Masten, A. (2001). Ordinary magic: Resilience processes in development, *American Psychologist*, 56(3), 227–238.

Nelson, C. A., Zeanah, C. A., Fox, N. A., Marshall, P. J., Smyke, A. T. and Guthrie, D. (2007). Cognitive recovery in socially deprived young children: The Bucharest Early Intervention Project, *Science*, 318(5858), 1937–1940.

Newman, T. (2004). *What Works in Building Resilience?* London: Jessica Kingsley Publishers.

Ofsted (2015). *Early Years: The Report of Her Majesty's Chief Inspector of Education, Children's Services and Skills*, Manchester: Ofsted.

Roberts, R. (2010). *Wellbeing from Birth*, London: Sage Publications.

Rochat, P. (2010). The innate sense of the body develops to become a public affair by 2–3 years, *Neuropsychologia*, 48(3), 738–745.

Rutter, M. (1987). Psychosocial resilience and protective mechanisms, *American Journal of Orthopsychiatry*, 57(3), 316–331.

Rutter, M., Beckett, C., Castle, J., Kreppner, J., Stevens, S. and Sonuga-Barke, E. (2009). *Policy and Practice Implications from the English and Romanian Adoptees (ERA) Study: Forty-five key questions*, London: British Association for Adoption and Fostering (BAAF).

Sameroff, A. J. (1991). The social context of development. In Woodhead, M., Carr, R. and Light, P. (eds.), *Becoming a Person (Child Development in Social Context 1)*, London: Routledge, 167–189.

Schaffer, H. R. (1996). *Social Development*, Oxford: Blackwell Publishers.

Smith, M. (2015). From adversity to buoyancy, *The Psychologist*, 28(9) 718–721.

Smith, R., Purdon, S., Schneider, V., La Valle, I., Wollny, I., Owen, R., Bryson, C., Mathers, S., Sylva, K. and Lloyd, E. (2009). *Early Education Pilot for Two Year Old Children Evaluation*. DCSF research report no. DCSF-RR134.

Sroufe, L. A., Egeland, B., Carson, A. and Collins, W. A. (2005). *The Development of the Person: The Minnesota Study of Risk and Adaptation from Birth to Adulthood*, New York: The Guildford Press.

Tizard, B. (1977). *Adoption: A second chance*, London: Open Books.

Wave Trust/DfE (2013). *Conception to Age 2 – the age of opportunity*, Surrey: Wave Trust.

Werner, E. E. (1989). High-risk children in young adulthood: A longitudinal study from birth to 32 years, *American Journal of Orthopsychiatry*, 59, 72–81.

Werner, E. E. (1993). *Risk, Resilience and Recovery: Perspectives from the Kauai longitudinal study of resilient children and youth*, New York: McGraw Hill.

Werner, E. E. and Smith, R. S. (1982). *Vulnerable but Invincible: A longitudinal study of resilient children and youth*, New York: McGraw Hill.

4

QUALITY FOR TWO-YEAR-OLDS

Verity Campbell-Barr

Introduction

In September 2013, the UK introduced free, quality, early education places for disadvantaged two-year-olds. The places built on longer-term policy trajectories focused on the importance of *quality* early years services for supporting the holistic development of children, alongside facilitating parental employment. The places for two-year-olds had been preceded by the introduction of free early years places for three- and four-year-olds (via a phased introduction of the places). Whilst attention to quality has long been a feature of early years policy, the two-year-olds funding differed from the three- and four-year-olds offer by including quality criteria to determine which settings were eligible to draw down the state funding to provide the places. Despite the introduction of the quality criteria, this is not to say that quality is an easily understood concept. In this chapter I consider both what quality is for early years services and who informs this, drawing on literature concerning the quality of early years services generically. I then consider whether there is something distinct when looking at quality for two-year-olds, drawing on empirical research to develop the discussion. The discussion is framed by a post-structuralist approach that seeks to question quality as a knowable and fixed entity, with the focus on the two-year-old funding illustrating how quality is relative to the needs of the child.

I refer throughout the chapter to early years services as a generic term, but I recognise that there are many debates on how best to refer to services for two-year-olds. The UK has a legacy of a split early childhood education and care model, whereby childcare was provided for children from birth to three years of age and early education for those of three years to school age. Whilst attempts have been made to create a more integrated (birth to school age) model, the split system has a lasting legacy of an association of care-based services for younger children and education-focussed ones for older children (Bennett, 2006; Moss, 2006). At a practical level, education and care are rarely divided and I know that many practitioners will identify with an approach that integrates both care and education, irrespective of age. However, how best to refer to the places for two-year-olds is important as it shapes how early years services are understood, such as whether their role and purpose is care or education focussed (see Chapter 5 for further discussion of terms used to refer to early years settings). The purpose of the funded places has implications for how quality is constructed. To help illustrate the interplay between constructions of early years services and quality, I begin with an overview of recent policy developments in the UK to provide a context for considering debates on quality and who and what has informed them.

Policy overview

The introduction of the National Childcare Strategy in 1998 (Department for Education and Employment, 1998) focussed policy efforts and interest on the quality, affordability and accessibility of early years services. The Strategy included broad-ranging initiatives aimed at increasing the provision of early years services, alongside incentivising parents to access them. The Strategy represented dual social investment agendas of supporting parental employment and recognising early years services as contributing to a child's holistic development (Campbell-Barr, 2015). The aims of the Strategy were not always perfect; targets for local authorities to secure sufficient early years places meant that often sufficiency came before quality. A prime example is the introduction of free early years places for three- and four-year-olds which, despite having a phased roll-out for the latter (with an initial targeting of places in disadvantaged areas), faced pressures to ensure sufficiency. The initial offer was for 12.5 hours, later extended to 15, with a gradual shift towards offering the free entitlement flexibly, whereby parents could spread the hours over a week or concentrate them in a few days to suit their needs. The focus on sufficiency and flexibility was complicated by a reliance on a mixed-market model of early years services involving the maintained and private, voluntary and independent sectors (PVI). In 2006, the Childcare Act (Great Britain, 2006) legislated for the maintained sector to be the last resort in the expansion of places, resulting in a state entitlement to early years services being reliant on the PVI sectors, despite concerns that a reliance on the market could have implications for the quality and sustainability of provision (Penn, 2009; Lloyd and Penn, 2010) and longstanding debates concerning the sufficiency of government funding for *quality* early years services.

The introduction of the free early years places for two-year-olds was more than just an extension of the three- and four-year-olds offer, as the services were targeted at disadvantaged children and families and settings also had to meet quality criteria pertaining to their Ofsted grade. This is not to ignore issues with sustainability and sufficiency, but the emphasis on quality reflected acknowledgement in policy of a growing body of research that demonstrates high-quality early years services as better placed to support development, particularly of children from disadvantaged backgrounds. Ofsted inspections were extended to the private and voluntary sector from 1998, with each of the countries that form the UK developing their own systems. Prior to this, inspections had been carried out at a local authority level, so the introduction of Ofsted symbolised a significant step in developing a *national* approach to the quality of early years services.

Ofsted provided a grade for the quality of the service. Initially, separate grades were provided for care and education based services, resulting in some settings being inspected twice, but now there is one sole grade of: Outstanding, Good, Requires Improvement or Inadequate. In 2014, Ofsted became the sole arbiter of quality, meaning that only the grades that they gave would be used to judge the quality of a setting to determine who would be eligible to draw down funding for the provision of early years places for two-year-olds. Prior to this local authorities had been able to develop local systems for monitoring quality to help supplement the grades given by Ofsted to guide support structures for local early years practitioners. Ofsted as the sole arbiter of quality faced criticism both in regard to general concerns about the inspection process and more specific ones about the needs of two-year-olds within early years settings. There have been questions of the objectivity of the inspections, concerns that inspections only provide a snapshot in time, and that inspectors do not always understand the intricacies of early years provision (Campbell-Barr, 2010; Ho et al., 2010). Further criticisms have been raised in regard to whether the inspection process is a supportive one that enables improvements in quality, with suggestions from the literature on schools that the process can be dependent on the individual inspector and how they manage themselves (Gilroy and Wilcox, 1997; Penn, 2002; Rosenthal, 2004). Whilst there is an inevitability that a national inspection system might be open to criticism, the concerns around whether the inspections sufficiently focussed on quality for two-year-olds are pertinent.

Mathers et al. (2012) explored the relationship between Ofsted grades and those of internationally recognised quality assessment tools ECERS-R (Early Childhood Environment Rating Scale for children two-and-a-half to five) and ITERS (Infant and Toddler Environment Rating Scale for children from birth to two and a half). As stated, Ofsted provides a grade of Outstanding, Good, Requires Improvement or Inadequate, whilst ECERS and ITERS use an observation framework with a series of different items against which a score can be provided. Mathers et al. found that whilst there was a relationship between Ofsted grades and ECERS scores, there was no relationship between Ofsted grades and ITERS scores. This difference suggests that Ofsted is more aligned to quality early years services for older children than those for two-year-olds. These findings should be treated with caution, however, as the purpose of Ofsted is not the same as that of ECERS and ITERS, but they do raise a question as to whether quality is different for children of different ages.

The inspection process was part of wider policy initiatives concerning the quality of early years provision, many of which were focussed upon pedagogical practices. Many of the developments were related to the early years curriculum and the various revisions to it, whilst simultaneously drawing attention to the policy objectives for early years services. The Early Years Foundation Stage (EYFS) (DfE, 2014) is the result of bringing together the earlier separate curricula of Birth to Three Matters and the Foundation Stage to create a comprehensive birth to five years of age curriculum that has been reviewed and amended over the years (see Robert-Holmes, 2012). Alongside the EYFS, the Early Years Foundation Stage Profile required practitioners to observe children in order to monitor children's development whilst also informing their pedagogical practice (Campbell-Barr, 2010). Observations have long been a feature of early years practice (Luff, 2014), the motivation being to deepen understandings of the child and their learning and to inform the development of pedagogical practice. Observations and reflective practice, whereby practitioners study their practice with an aim to improve their work, constitute core principles of high-quality early years services, but there are concerns that they are increasingly becoming part of accountability structures. For example, within the Ofsted framework practitioners are expected to undertake a self-evaluation, but the formal requirement shifts observation and reflection away from being a part of the epistemological base of early years practice to being a surveillance tool, a way of monitoring early years practice (see Campell-Barr and Leeson, 2016). Observations become a means of reporting on children's learning rather than a tool for informing practice, with further concerns that the datafication of the early years subverts early years pedagogical principles of focussing on the needs of the child (Roberts-Holmes, 2014).

The accountability structures are evident in other quality initiatives, such as the upskilling of the workforce (considered in more depth in Chapter 7) and the adoption of managerial and entrepreneurial-based models over a more ethical construct of early years practitioners (Dahlberg and Moss, 2005; Osgood, 2010). Further, the upskilling agenda highlights how much of early years policy has been done *to* early years practitioners, rather than *with* them (Campbell-Barr, 2015). The positioning of early years practice and practitioners as objects to be moulded in quality initiatives demonstrates the increased expectations of early years services and those who work in them, whilst highlighting the tensions between quality as accountability and more philosophical constructs.

Debates on quality

The policy interest in the quality of early years services reflects an evolution in research into early years services, with both having consequences for how quality has been conceptualised. Research studies initially considered the effects of maternal and non-maternal care on child development (see Chapter 3 for a discussion of children bonding with non-maternal caregivers), leading to an appreciation of the importance of the quality of care. Studies then shifted focus to identify features of quality that were associated with positive child outcomes, with more recent studies adopting a more ecological approach by acknowledging that the child's and their family's circumstances also influence child development (Fenech, 2011). Within the ecological model, interest was focussed on whether early years services had different outcomes for children with different characteristics, leading to the identification of early years services as particularly advantageous for the development of children from socio-economically deprived backgrounds. The prevailing influence of child development theories to inform research into the quality of early years services has been heavily criticised. Frequently there is a presumed linearity of child development and a tendency to classify and normalise what is seen as 'typical' development (Dahlberg and Moss, 2005). The classifying and normalising enable the 'abnormal' (those children who do not attain the prescribed levels at the expected ages and stages) to be identified, with high-quality early years services becoming the way to fix and normalise children through the application of the right techniques. Framing this normalising approach within a social equality agenda enables it to be seen as a form of social justice, whereby all children are provided with the maximum opportunity to improve their life chances – and I would not dispute that early years services have a lot to offer children. However, the targeting of disadvantaged children in the early years places for two-year-olds initiative also has an economic turn, whereby the normalising process is only of concern because, as Penn (2012) pointed out, children from disadvantaged backgrounds cost the state money.

Both the economic interest and the focus on the role of early years services in supporting child development are important for informing understandings of quality, as quality becomes regarded as an early years service that achieves the desired developmental and economic goals. The economic model is largely informed by human capital theory, whereby an investment in the early years is regarded as an investment in the foundations for children's later learning. I do not dispute the important function of early years services for supporting children's development, but I question the constructions of child development within economic frameworks. Human Capital theory is framed by recognition of the role of education in developing the knowledge, skills and other attributes of individuals and is reflective of a lifelong learning agenda. Early studies around human capital did not include early years services, but as understandings of early years services developed it was appreciated that they not only had an important function in supporting learning, but also that they were a good source of investment, because they would reduce the need for additional educational and welfare support later in a child's life. There are criticisms of the role of Human Capital theory in the early years due to questions about the global relevance and representativeness of the research studies that have informed economic justification for investment in early years services and because of questions about what might not be captured in these assessments of value (Campbell-Barr, 2012; Penn, 2012). Interestingly, Heckman, who was influential in developing understandings of value in the provision of early years services, has also issued caution regarding how value is determined. His concern is that increasingly concepts of value are being reduced down to knowledge and skills and are failing to capture the holistic nature of the 'other attributes' of child development that are supposed to be present within human capital perspectives (Heckman, 2000). The implications are that quality is understood as those services which best

Quality for two-year-olds **41**

develop children's knowledge and skills, particularly those children from disadvantaged backgrounds, something that is arguably present in the accountability models discussed earlier.

Understanding high-quality early years services as part of a normalising process underpinned by an economic agenda also reflects a deficit model of children and childhood. The two-year-olds targeted by the funded places initiative are children who have been labelled as lacking in some way. The deficit model is based on what the children do not have, rather than celebrating what they do. There are two issues in regard to framing quality early years services as part of a normalising process; the first is that in order to be able to assess the effectiveness of early years services and determine if they offer value for money, there is a privileging of approaches to quality and child development that can be measured and assessed, and the second is the construction of what are seen as the desirable norms. The focus on measurement reflects modernist approaches to quality, whereby there is a rational and positivistic approach that privileges what can be measured and assessed in an objective and reliable way. Within modernity the world is regarded as ordered, with knowable features that can be identified and researched (Dahlberg et al., 2013). Research thus becomes a way of knowing something and gives rise to discursive truths – things that are known and believed about the social world. In the case of quality early years services, high quality is now accepted as being important and many features that I have already identified are a part of this, such as the workforce and the curriculum. Discursive truths create particular ways of knowing and talking about early years services and these ideas become so deeply engrained that often there is no attempt to stop and think about them. If I return to the example of child development and its supposed linearity, there is an assumption that all children will progress and develop at the same rate and that there is a normal stage (an enlightenment goal) to be reached. The normal will be socially constructed features of desirable child outcomes, such as knowledge and skills, but features that are less valued and/or harder to measure become lost in constructions of child development and quality early years services.

Post-structuralism challenges the presumed certainty of modernism and encourages individuals to ask questions in order to deconstruct where understandings of quality come from (Campbell-Barr and Leeson, 2016). For example, to return to the discussion of the evolution of research on quality early years services, it is possible to identify the legacy of understandings of child development informing how quality is understood. However, child development has interplayed with economic theory and the ideologies of policy-makers, whereby some features of child development become privileged, such as knowledge and skills within human capital perspectives. Quality becomes about a notion that early years services are to achieve X, so we need Y in order to do this, what Ball (2008) has framed as a 'what-works' approach to policy-making. In what-works policy-making, modernist approaches to assessments of quality are favoured for their supposed objectivity and reliability in determining quality early years services. A what-works approach to early years services has become prominent in England, with debates taking place about the role of early years services to ensure that children are 'school ready'. However, how school ready is defined will have a consequence for how quality is understood. Let's consider for a moment a model of 'school ready' based on social cohesion as opposed to one focussed on a child's knowledge of phonics; the two would provide different understandings of quality early years services. Post-structuralism enables a critical deconstruction of who and what are shaping understandings of quality and opens up alternative understandings of quality. The adoption of a more critical approach to early years pedagogy requires a more critically aware workforce, who consider and reflect on the challenges of daily practice, rather than seeking to apply the right techniques at the right times to achieve the right outcomes (Dahlberg and Moss, 2005; Mac Naughton, 2005). Post-structuralist approaches enable an inspection process such as Ofsted or the quality scales of ECERS and ITERS to be seen as pertaining to just one form of quality – just one form of truth, with a need to go beyond these truths in order to consider other possibilities (Dahlberg et al., 2013).

Understanding quality for two-year-olds

Research that has looked specifically at the quality of early years services for two-year-olds is limited. With both research and policy having historically focussed on three- and four-year-olds, this may have implications for the discursive truths of quality early years services. Soukakou et al. (2014) conducted a review of the evidence on quality for two-year-olds and acknowledged that understandings of quality are informed by how two-year-olds are understood, how they are seen to learn and what they are seen to need to learn. Quality for two-year-olds is underpinned by ideas of children as confident and capable learners, with their learning being framed by the child development discourse referred to earlier and increasing evidence from neuroscience (Soukakou et al., 2014). Embedded in these are understandings of the child's need for secure attachments and their developing sense of self (see Chapter 3), the importance of their language development and an appreciation of them as physical learners. Given this, it is perhaps unsurprising that the features of good quality that Soukakou et al. identified include stable relationships, play-based approaches and opportunities for physical movement, child-led learning, the need for language support and stimulating environments. Soukakou et al.'s review highlights that understandings of quality have implications for pedagogical practice, with a clear need for skilled and knowledgeable staff to develop this practice.

Mathers and Smees (2014) undertook an international literature review focussed on working with children under three years, and whilst noting the limited literature available, identified that stable relationships and interactions with sensitive and responsive staff, play-based approaches where children can lead their own learning, support for communication and opportunities for being physically active were all important when working with two-year-olds. The findings of Soukakou et al. and Mathers and Smees echo Dalli's (2014) review. Dalli's discussion of quality for younger children is also helpful for understanding how different perspectives

Quality for two-year-olds **43**

of quality inform how it is understood; one is framed by the modernist approach referred to earlier whereby research into the quality of early years services is informed by multi-level modelling and statistical analysis, and the other entails more critical and philosophical debate. The latter provided the framework for the research undertaken with early years representatives to consider understandings of quality early years services for two-year-olds (Georgeson et al., 2014).

The views of stakeholders

The limited evidence base on quality for two-year-olds is not surprising given that policy agendas had previously focussed on three- and four-year-olds. Questions therefore remained as to whether quality for two-year-olds is in some way different from that for three- and four-year-olds. As part of Georgeson et al.'s wider research study (Georgeson et al., 2014), 13 interviews were undertaken with professionals who had a role in supporting early years providers, such as local authority officers and charity organisations, to consider their understandings of quality in early years services for two-year-olds. Through either face-to-face or telephone interviews, participants were asked to consider two core questions: what constitutes quality for two-year-olds and what is the role of the workforce in relation to this? However, whilst two core questions were planned, it was evident that respondents did not see them as separate, instead viewing the two as inextricably linked, with answers to the former simultaneously covering responses to the latter. The analysis that follows is based on the themes that were identified within these key informant interviews and, whilst I sought to identify them through a grounded approach to the analysis (Creswell, 2002), I am conscious that the analysis may well be shaped by the discursive construction of quality in early years services and an expectation that particular themes will emerge. Equally, the analysis can be viewed as illustrative of how the discursive construction of early years quality is shaping the ways in which the key informants discussed quality for two-year-olds. The analysis begins by considering the relationship between quality and the workforce, including leadership and management and questions of the ideal qualification level, before going on to consider child development and work with families.

Firstly, it is important to stress the commitment of those interviewed to the quality of early years services and that many regarded quality for two-year-olds as being a part of the wider picture of quality. Therefore, for them quality for two-year-olds was not different or distinct, but (as for all children) responsive to the child's needs.

The workforce

As stated, it was clear that for all key informants the quality of early years services was inextricably linked with the workforce and whilst this included a discussion of qualifications, it also recognised the importance of relational skills, skills that might come from outside of qualifications and leadership and management. Nearly all key informants were committed to Level Three qualifications being a minimum

44   Verity Campbell-Barr

requirement (see Chapter 7 for more details on qualification levels), but many also had concerns about whether the qualifications that were current at the time of the research were fit for purpose. Key informants raised questions as to how robust the assessment processes were, whether those undertaking the assessments were adequately qualified and if there was parity between employment- and college-based pathways. Early years qualifications had recently been reviewed in England (Nutbrown, 2012) and many respondents referred to this review process and raised questions about some of the outcomes of the review, such as whether GCSEs in Maths, Science and English were really necessary for working with young children.

The discussions demonstrated respondents' passion and commitment to ensuring that those working with young children were well prepared for their working role, but also revealed considerable debate as to how best to achieve this. Some key informants were very clear in advocating a Level Six (degree) qualification, partly to ensure parity between different sectors (as at the time of writing only those working in the maintained sector are required to hold a Level Six qualification), but also because qualification at Level Six was seen as more likely to uphold the reflective principles discussed earlier. However, all key informants believed that those working in early years services should have a qualification that focussed on the appropriate age range and was underpinned by theories on child development. Whilst the highlighting of an appropriate age range was occasionally targeted as a criticism of practitioners working in schools who might not have covered working with two-year-olds in their degree, the second point reflects the extent to which child development is deeply engrained in understandings of early years practice.

Many local authorities had offered additional training prior to the introduction of the two-year-old places to consider the development of a two-year-old. There was a strong feeling that those working with two-year-olds needed to know about how to respond to the needs of the child and understand their abilities.

> *They need to understand how two-year-olds learn, how they like to learn, the sorts of character of their learning, their desire for learning.*
> (KI:3 Trainer, Consultant and National Charity Representative)

> *It's the skills and the way staff work and engage with children, so then having that good understanding of child development and the particular needs of two-year-olds.*
> (KI:11 Policy Officer, National Charity Representative)

As Chapters 2 and 3 have indicated, two-year-olds are experiencing a rich and rapid stage of development, but there can also be misconceptions of their development, associated with negative connotations, such as the 'terrible twos' (see Chapter 5). Further, whilst key informants did not articulate details about their understandings of child development (and nor was this something that I looked to explore in depth with them), they did express the need to appreciate the complexities of child development. In particular, key informants identified that, given the targeted nature of the funding for two-year-olds, often children came from complex backgrounds or had additional needs that would require practitioners' sensitivity and ability to support their development.

The environment

The focus on child development within understandings of quality was also apparent in the frequent references to the pedagogical principles of play-based, child-led and educare-focussed approaches; these were to be supported by a pedagogical environment that was stimulating and appropriate for the developmental needs of two-year-olds, with nearly all advocating the importance of having free-flow access to the outside. The discussion of the environment included providing stimulating resources appropriate to the developmental needs of two-year-olds, including outdoor resources, recognising that some of the children that were being targeted within the two-year-old offer would not have access to the outdoors within their home environment.

Working with families

The connection to the home learning environment reflected a wider appreciation that high-quality early years practice includes working with families, which included the recognition that, while much needed, the targeted nature of the funding could mean that work with the families of two-year-olds could be particularly challenging.

> *There is a large amount of work there with families and being able to engage with the family… the child can be settled, but the family has difficulties that impact on the child being able to take up the place.*
>
> (KI:10 Trainer, National Charity Representative)

Key informants from local authorities acknowledged that the complex needs of two-year-olds and their families often meant that there was a need for additional support within the setting. This support could involve drawing on the expertise of the Special Educational Needs Coordinator (SENCO), getting advice from local authority personnel or attending additional training, but key informants also identified that working with families often entailed partnership working (see Chapters 8 and 11).

Piecing together the quality puzzle

The key informant interviews did not present quality for two-year-olds as distinct from quality for other age groups, but rather identified that it required some degree of specialist knowledge of the developmental needs of two-year-olds. Key informants also identified that the targeting of the funding for two-year-olds meant that the children and families could have additional needs and/or complex lives and, whilst this did not alter their overall conception of quality, could realign the way in which quality is focussed. For example, more emphasis might be placed on working with families in relation to a child's additional needs or seeking to support their self-confidence (see Chapters 3 and 11). Exploring concepts of quality in relation to the two-year-olds offer has demonstrated a degree of individualising the concept of quality within daily practice. However, I would argue that despite the notion of individualising, there are some deeply engrained features of quality that have come to reflect discursive truths as to what constitutes quality in early years practice and are evident in literature, policy and in the discussions with key informants. For example, the importance of the workforce, the connection to child development and a need for a relational pedagogy that is child-centred and play-based are all commonly referred to in discussions of quality early years practice. I would not look to dispute these aspects of quality in early years practice, but I would argue that there is a need to explore what is really meant by each of these terms, particularly in light of the comments from the key informants that suggest that working with disadvantaged two-year-olds requires all of these areas, but in a 'plus' model – all these and something more depending on the specific needs of the child. The example of working with disadvantaged two-year-olds indicates the individualising of quality, that quality in early years practice is not the same for all children. Yes, there are common features to high-quality early years practice, as has been identified in this chapter but, as Georgeson discusses in Chapter 6, practitioners are constantly and unconsciously negotiating these different features of quality in careful and skilful ways to inform their pedagogical practice and respond to the needs of different children. Quality is therefore not a fixed entity, but something to be negotiated in daily practice to respond to the needs of the children in early years settings.

Modernistic models of quality that seek to observe, measure and treat quality as a knowable entity are problematic, as are associated ways of knowing about a child's development, as both presume an enlightenment goal to be reached. The underlying assumption is that quality is a fixed point, such as achieving Outstanding in an Ofsted inspection, but I would suggest that what was evident from our key informants is that quality is understood as variable, to be adapted to meet the needs of the children and families with whom early years practitioners are working. Modernist assessments of quality could be accused of creating uniformity, but one of the most enjoyable aspects of visiting early years settings is seeing the variety of ways in which practitioners succeed in adapting the common features of quality identified here to suit the needs of the children and families they work with. The funded two-year-old offer has highlighted how complex working with children and families can be; there can therefore be no one-size-fits-all approach to quality. The temptation to identify knowable (commonly referenced) features can be hard to resist, but I would argue that those working to support early years practitioners (as well as the practitioners themselves) are questioning what is meant by quality and recognising its variability (see Chapter 8 for practitioners discussing their approaches to providing high-quality education and care for two-year-olds).

Quality for two-year-olds **47**

I would suggest that the next stage for developing understandings of quality is to ask questions about the common features that have been identified.

Questions

Consider your own definition of quality; what are the features that you would look for? Why is it that you consider these features as particularly important? What challenges and enablers can you identify within your own practice in delivering *quality* early childhood education and care? What can you learn from the enablers to help overcome the challenges?

Further reading

Dalli, C. (2014). *Occasional paper 4: Quality for babies and toddlers in early years settings*: TACTYC. http://tactyc.org.uk/wp-content/uploads/2014/04/Occ-Paper-4-Prof-Carmen-Dalli.pdf. (Accessed on: 08/08/2017)

This paper is helpful for considering different theoretical perspectives on 'quality' whilst also focussing specifically on younger children. In reading the paper, it is worth considering whether you see quality for babies and toddlers as distinct from quality for children of other ages or as part of the same pack.

References

Ball, S. J. (2008). *The education debate*. Bristol: Policy Press.

Bennett, J. (2006). New policy conclusions from starting strong II: An update on the OECD early childhood policy reviews. *European Early Childhood Education Research Journal*, 14(2), 141–156.

Campbell-Barr, V. (2010). *Providing a context for looking at quality and value in early years education*. Report to the Office for National Statistics Measuring Outcomes for Public Service Users. Newport: Office for National Statistics.

Campbell-Barr, V. (2012). Early years education and the value for money folklore. *European Early Childhood Education Research Journal*, 20(3), 423–437.

Campbell-Barr, V. (2015). The research, policy and practice triangle in early childhood education and care, in Parker-Rees, R. and Lesson, C. (eds.), *Early childhood studies*. Exeter: Learning Matters, 234–248.

Campbell-Barr, V., and Leeson, C. (2016). *Quality and leadership in the early years*. London: Sage.

Creswell, J. W. (2002). *Educational research: Planning, conducting, and evaluating quantitative and qualitative research*. Upper Saddle River, NJ: Prentice Hall.

Dahlberg, G., and Moss, P. (2005). *Ethics and politics in early childhood education*. London: Routledge/Falmer.

Dahlberg, G., Pence, A., and Moss, P. (2013). *Beyond quality in early childhood education and care: Languages of evaluation*. 3rd ed. London: Routledge.

Dalli, C. (2014). *Occasional paper 4: Quality for babies and toddlers in early years settings*. TACTYC. http://tactyc.org.uk/wp-content/uploads/2014/04/Occ-Paper-4-Prof-Carmen-Dalli.pdf (Accessed on: 08/08/2017).

Department for Education (DfE) (2014). *Statutory Framework for the Early Years Foundation Stage*. London: DfE.

Department for Education and Employment (DfEE) (1998). *Meeting the childcare challenge: A framework and consultation document*. London: DfEE.

Fenech, M. (2011). An analysis of the conceptualisation of 'quality' in early childhood education and care empirical research: Promoting 'blind spots' as foci for future research. *Contemporary Issues in Early Childhood*, 12(2), 102–117.

Georgeson, J., Campbell-Barr, V., Boag-Munroe, G., Mathers, S., Caruso, F., and Parker-Rees, R. (2014). *Two-year-olds in England: An exploratory study*. TACTYC. Available at http://tactyc.org.uk/research/ (Accessed on: 09/08/2017).

Gilroy, P., and Wilcox, B. (1997). Ofsted, criteria and the nature of social understanding: A Wittgensteinian critique of the practice of educational judgement. *British Journal of Educational Studies*, 45(1), 22–38.

Great Britain. (2006). *Childcare Act 2006: Elizabeth II*. London: Stationery Office.

Heckman, J. (2000). *Invest in the very young*. Chicago, IL: Ounce of Prevention Fund and the University of Chicago Harris School of Public Policy Studies.

Ho, D., Campbell-Barr, V., and Leeson, C. (2010). Quality improvement in early years settings in Hong Kong and England. *International Journal of Early Years Education*, 18(3), 243–258.

Lloyd, E., and Penn, H. (2010). Why do childcare markets fail? Comparing England and the Netherlands. *Public Policy Research*, 17(1), 42–48.

Luff, P. (2014). Necessary paperwork: Observation and assessment in the Early Years Foundation Stage, in Moyles, J., Payler, J., and Georgeson, J. (eds.), *Early years foundations: Critical issues*. Maidenhead, Berkshire: McGraw-Hill, 30–40.

Mac Naughton, G. (2005). *Doing Foucault in early childhood studies: Applying poststructural ideas*. London: Routledge.

Mathers, S., Singler, R., and Karemaker, A. (2012). *Improving quality in the early years: A comparison of perspectives and measures*. London: Daycare Trust and Oxford: University of Oxford. www.education.ox.ac.uk/wordpress/wp-content/uploads/2012/03/Early-Years-Quality-Mathers-et-al-Final-Report-2012.pdf (Accessed on: 28/09/2017)

Mathers, S., and Smees, R. (2014). *Quality and inequality: Do three- and four-year-olds in deprived areas experience lower quality early years provision?* London: Nuffield Foundation. www.nuffieldfoundation.org/sites/default/files/files/Quality_inequality_childcare_mathers_29_05_14.pdf (Accessed on: 06/08/2017).

Moss, P. (2006). Farewell to childcare? *National Institute Economic Review*, 195(1), 70–83.

Nutbrown, C. (2012). *Foundations for quality: The independent review of early education and childcare qualifications: Final report*. DFE-00068 2012. www.gov.uk/government/uploads/system/uploads/attachment_data/file/175463/Nutbrown-Review.pdf (Accessed on: 08/08/2017).

Osgood, J. (2010). Reconstructing professionalism in ECEC: The case for the critically reflective emotional professional. *Early Years: An International Journal of Research and Development*, 30(2), 119–133.

Penn, H. (2002). 'Maintains a good pace to lessons': Inconsistencies and contextual factors affecting OFSTED inspections of nursery schools. *British Educational Research Journal*, 28(6), 879–888.

Penn, H. (2009). International perspectives on quality in mixed economies of childcare. *National Institute Economic Review*, 207(1), 83–89.

Penn, H. (2012). Shaping the future: How human capital arguments about investment in early childhood are being (mis)used in poor countries, in Yelland, N. (ed.), *Contemporary perspectives on early childhood education*. Maidenhead, Berkshire: Open University Press, 49–65.

Roberts-Holmes, G. (2012). 'It's the bread and butter of our practice': Experiencing the Early Years Foundation Stage. *International Journal of Early Years Education*, 20(1), 30–42.

Roberts-Holmes, G. (2014). The 'datafication' of early years pedagogy: 'If the teaching is good, the data should be good and if there's bad teaching, there is bad data.' *Journal of Education Policy*, 30(3), 302–315.

Rosenthal, L. (2004). Do school inspections improve school quality? Ofsted inspections and school examination results in the UK. *Economics of Education Review*, 23(2), 143–151.

Soukakou, E., Ereky-Stevens, K., Sylva, K., Eisenstadt, N., and Mathers, S. (2014). *Sound foundations: A review of the research evidence on quality of early childhood education and care for children under three: Implications for policy and practice*. London: Sutton Trust.

5

TALKING ABOUT TWO-YEAR-OLDS

The potential impact of early years discourses on identity formation

Gill Boag-Munroe

> The way you see people is the way you treat them and the way you treat them is what they become.
>
> (Attr. Goethe)

> 'the object of investigation is not people [...] but rather the thought-language with which they refer to reality and their view of the world.'
>
> (Freire, 1970: 78)

Introduction

It is important to remember that children often overhear interactions between adults and that they are likely to try to interpret those interactions in relation to themselves. Let me tell you a story. There was once a little girl – let's call her Poppy. In this story, Poppy's family were out walking one day, but Poppy wasn't enjoying the walk. She was tired and wanted to go home for a sleep. Poppy's parents didn't understand this, so she tried to tell them again in the only way she knew how: with a loud voice and tears. Mr and Mrs Smith were passing at the time and noticed Poppy, and heard her parents telling her off. A little while later, when Poppy's family were returning from their walk, the Smiths saw Poppy and exclaimed, 'Oh look! It's that terrible Poppy.' Poppy, who had behaved perfectly on the rest of the walk, shouted 'I not terrible Poppy', burst into tears and stamped her feet in a huge puddle, soaking Mr and Mrs Smith.

My aim in this chapter is to provoke thinking about how adults working with two-year-olds talk or write about them; actions and words can betray how we are thinking and young children can pick up on and react to how they are spoken about. Much has been written about working with two-year-old children in terms of how this age group learns; how to organise settings and learning for them; how to manage their behaviour; and the perceived social, economic and educational benefits of including them in early years settings (see Chapter 4). Yet little attention is paid to how the language used in these discussions can shape possibilities for conceptualising children, and thereby affect the ways in which practitioners and parents engage with them and meet what adults perceive to be their needs. Furthermore, when two-year-old children hear people talking about them, they pick up what is (and what is not) said *about* them as well as *to* them, internalising their interpretations of adult perspectives of who and what they are. How, for example, might they feel when they hear a story in which an older sibling's birthday will be spoiled by the behaviour of her two-year-old brother and sister (Reich and Bracken, 1984)? Or how do they feel when they hear adults around them talking about the 'terrible twos' and their tantrums?

In the first part of the chapter, I briefly survey how two-year-olds develop their understanding of language in interactions and then go on to consider how, because language and thought are intimately connected, language plays a part in the construction of children's identities through their interpretation of what they hear. Along the way, I highlight the complexity of how two-year-olds are described in some of the literature, including illustrative examples from government policy documents relating to early years practice, and also consider how the coincidence of an emergent theory of mind, developing language skills, and participation in different contexts helps to shape the child's identity. I reflect on how, currently, certain ways of talking about children might pathologise two-year-old behaviour and mislead parents and practitioners into interactions that can add to frustration and lead to self-fulfilling prophecies, as Poppy's story showed. Finally, I conclude with rather more questions than I have answered, concerning how practitioners and parents might navigate their way through this minefield of language to avoid damage to fragile identities. I argue that adults working with two-year-olds should pay closer attention to the ways in which the language, routines and environments of early childhood contexts can set up expectations about children and families and the sorts of things they can do and say.

The developing two-year-old

At the age of about two years, children are beginning to develop a theory of mind, which is intimately connected to their developing language skills (Astington and Edward, 2010). As their language develops, so they become aware that others use language in different ways, though they are not yet able to discriminate the nuances of language. As children move from the family circle to nursery and to other social environments, they encounter new communities of practice (Lave and Wenger, 1991), each with their own ways of using language. The more the child is exposed to different forms of language, the more she can build subtle concepts, and the more she can become aware of others and her own interaction with them. It is from this interaction, and the language heard in it, that the child begins to learn about the limits of her agency within different social and cultural communities.

The concept of 'community of practice' is a useful one for understanding how children can move from being a novice in a community to full participation, particularly when considered in conjunction with Rogoff et al.'s (1993) concept of 'guided participation'. This concept is concerned not just with the face-to-face interaction between people as they take part in an activity, but also with the side-by-side joint participation that features in many of the activities of normal daily life. Rogoff et al. explain further that participants can be guided as much by cultural and social values inherent in an activity as by the words and actions of other people taking part, and will participate through observation as well as through direct involvement. These concepts do not, however, allow an adequate investigation of how the child's interactions with those people she encounters in her different worlds contribute to the construction of an identity for herself. For this, I turn to the ideas of Holland et al. (1998) and, in particular, their concepts of 'figured worlds' and 'spaces of authorship'. Figured worlds are spaces in which the imaginary is actualised (Holland et al., 1998). They offer spaces of authorship, possibilities for exploring who we are, and what we can do, in relation to other people. In a figured world, the figures can negotiate how they can act, and how they will construct meaning:

> A figured world is peopled by the figures, characters and types who carry out its tasks and who also have styles of interacting within, distinguishable perspectives on, and orientations to it,
>
> (Holland et al., 1998: 51)

Urrieta (2007) understands figured worlds as spaces where 'people "figure" who they are through the activities and in relation to the social types that populate these figured worlds, and in social relationships with those who perform these worlds' (Urrieta, 2007: 108). So, just as children might create imaginary worlds in which they practise ways of being (see Parker-Rees's account of different ways of being Mama in Chapter 2), so adults also create imaginary worlds which they actualise as types of ways of being (e.g. nursery, family, academia).

The literature on child development (e.g. Gopnik et al., 2001; Hardman, 2012) points to the age of about two years as the time when children's language development accelerates. Early language tends to be concerned with labelling objects, people, actions and events ('doggie gone'; 'want sweetie'; 'daddy play'), but, as Parker-Rees points out in Chapter 2, labels for these objects, people, actions and events can be very much tied to context. Figured worlds are populated by objects and people from a range of different social and cultural backgrounds who overlap with other figured worlds from which they draw their language and concepts, as well as their understandings of how artefacts are used. Language use for objects/persons/actions does not always match exactly across worlds; families often have their own words for everyday activities and two-year-olds soon find out that their words for toilet/grandparent/pet are different from those used by other people at nursery. It is from these experiences of difference and sameness that the two-year-old begins to develop their sense of who and what they are. Holland et al. have drawn on the work of Bakhtin to develop their understanding of how identities develop in particular kinds of social practice:

> The meaning we make of ourselves is, in Bakhtin's terms, 'authoring the self', and the site at which this authoring occurs is a space defined by the inter-relationship of differentiated 'vocal' perspectives on the social world.
>
> (Holland et al., 1998: 173)

Holland et al. (1998: 282) argue that it is the 'mixture of the perspective of the "I" and the words of others [which] create the contours of Bakhtin's contribution to our ideas of selves and identities'; within figured worlds, the child comes into contact with a range of voices speaking in a variety of genres, dialects, registers and discourses (in Bakhtin's word, heteroglossia), which the two-year-old child is just learning to understand as reflecting ways of being different from her own. At this stage of development, however, the child's language skills are not sufficiently developed to engage fully in conversations with someone speaking from another perspective, or to understand that the language in use is not always about the child and her world. Where words are understood, the child may use them to make meaning about herself and who she is; if, however, there are no adults available to the child within a zone of proximal development (Vygotsky, 1981) to mediate meaning for the child within that space of authoring, this can lead to confusion and misinterpretation.

I turn now to discussing the vital relationship between language and thinking which underpins the three strands of my argument: that adults' choice of language is influenced by particular ways of thinking about children and families which they have picked up during their personal and working lives; that children, hearing language they do not fully understand, may nonetheless use what they hear to shape what they think about themselves and who they are; and that practitioners should be mindful of the possibility that aspects of these identities may be troublesome (Jonsson and Williams, 2013).

Relationship between language and thinking

In order to access how a person understands their reality, one approach might be to examine the language they choose to describe it. Vanderbroeck et al. (2010) draw on Freire's (1970: 139) argument that 'the object of investigation is not people [...] but rather the thought-language with which they refer to reality and their view of the world'. The relationship between words and meaning can point to how someone is thinking (Boag-Munroe, 2004). Derry (2009), drawing on Vygotsky (1986), also highlights the dialectic (or the complex interaction between opposing concepts) between language and thought, arguing that 'language structures and constitutes thought, rather than merely expressing it' (p. 113). That is not to say that language and thought are identical, only that they are intimately connected. For Vygotsky, thought comes into existence because of language, whereas for Derry, meanings are developed through the dialectic of thought and language. So the choices we make from the language tools at our disposal can reveal the mental processes and concepts that we use to construct and shape the world we live in, in the same way that our decisions about material actions shape our environment. Exploring the language used across practice, policy-making and individual work with the child may, therefore, be helpful in clarifying how we understand what being a two-year-old means.

Bakhtin introduced the idea of polyphony – how the words used by a person are shaped by how those same words have been used by others now and in the past – and heteroglossia – the different ways or patterns of speaking, often called discourses, within a single language, which reflect the ideology of the speaker in the context in which they are speaking (Bakhtin, 1981). Children are 'engaged in a heteroglossic world' as they take on different roles in small world and role play (Cohen, 2009: 331). Adults talking to children, as early years practitioners or as parents, draw on a range of sources for the language they use within their interactions with each other and with children. Early years practice can be characterised by a 'rich polyphony of voices, creating many different stories out of a diversity of paradigms, theories and contexts' (Moss, 2015: 1). Practitioners engage in heteroglossia, stepping into and out of several discourses during each working day, or even in the course of one conversation, according to the figured world they see themselves entering. The ways in which they think about two-year-olds might therefore shift as they move in and out of different discourses. The discourses we choose to step into can shape how we think and act. Wagner and Einarsdottir (2006) draw attention to how discourses contain terms that point to the fundamental philosophy and ideology of our practice. In particular, they contrast the preferred, generic US term 'pre-school' for out-of-home care for children with the Icelandic preferred use of the word 'playschool', a word which points to the importance of play to children not yet of school age within the Icelandic Early Childhood tradition. Similarly, the Danes adopt the word 'kindergarten' because it specifically avoids associations with concepts relating to school: Danish pedagogues avoid referring to learning spaces for children under six-years-old as 'school' as they feel that such young children should not be in school-like institutions (p. 8).

Bronfenbrenner's (1979) ecological model of context can be used to explore understandings of the child from the outer circle of context inwards (see Figure 5.1) to show how dominant discourses of 'quality and high returns' (Moss, 2014: 3; see also Chapter 4) percolate downwards to the child rather than upwards, and the extent to which practice might thereby be shaped by policy rather than through collaboration between parents, practitioners, theorists and policy-makers. This appears to be at odds with the child-centred approaches espoused by early years practitioners (see Chapters 6, 7 and 8 for examples of such approaches).

It is these kinds of discourse features to which we need to attend in early years practice, to ensure that our philosophies, understandings, language and actions are aligned, rather than being haphazard and confusing. This will help to create coherent spaces in which children can learn who they are in these vital early years of life.

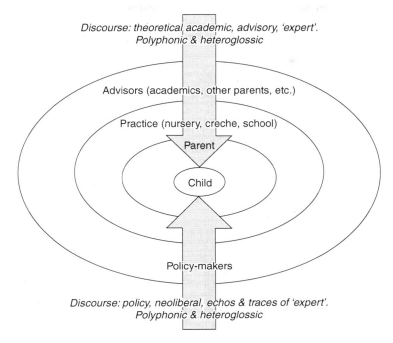

FIGURE 5.1 The child in an ecology of discourse

Textual explorations

To develop a broad-brush appreciation of some of the discourses drawn on by adults when they talk about children at this phase of development, I explored documents that gave guidance on how practitioners should work with two-year-olds, and also carried out a simple internet search for websites which used the keywords 'parental advice two-year-olds', 'terrible twos' and 'terrific twos'. Documents relating to early years education can be grouped into four broad categories: policy documents, written by policy-makers to an anticipated audience of practitioners; practitioner documents, usually written by or for those working with two-year-olds and drawing on practitioner discourses; and research documents, which draw on the discourses of the intended audience, usually policy-makers, researchers or practitioners. Alongside these documents sit internet texts which might be blogs or advice pages intended for either parents or practitioners. Here we will consider just policy documents and parental advice.

Policy documents

Moss (2014) believes that the stories we tell ourselves are important to the way that we 'weave reality'. He investigates the stories that are told about early childhood education, pointing to the language and concepts used to tell them, and challenges the 'dominant discourses in early childhood' (p. 1). He suggests that there are two dominant stories: TINA (There Is No Alternative) and DONA (Dictatorship Of No Alternative); and that the stories are of markets, quality and high returns, told within a metanarrative of neoliberalism. He sees the stories as stultifying, and argues for the possibility of transformative change.

It is not difficult to identify the neoliberal discourse running through government documents, shaping thinking about the aims and purposes of early years practice, and being transmitted, through analytical and explanatory texts, to practitioners and media. Within the illustrative papers I drew on, which outline policy aims and statutory directives, such as the report on early education research priorities (DfE, 2014), there are discourses of the market and of disadvantage which reflect a mechanistic and technocratic position, focusing on opportunities and solutions, markets, expansion and 'what works'. The language is of targets, development and developmental delay, feeding into a school-readiness discourse. We find words such as 'deliver', 'supply', 'demand', 'drive' and 'market' sitting alongside descriptor-and-nominalisation formulae of 'quality provision', 'effective teaching' or 'good practice'. The descriptors themselves tend to be empty words, meaning whatever the user wants them to mean: for the practitioner, trying to get hold of these slippery words so that meaning can be extracted is very difficult. Indeed, Wild et al. (2015) carried out a discourse analysis of two key early years reports (the Nutbrown Review and More Great Childcare) and found similarities in word frequency but subtle differences in how these words were used 'politically and ideologically' (p. 242) and which affected their meaning.

In policy discussions, childcare is often portrayed as a problem to be solved. The prevailing idea of 'market' suggests cattle or auctions, with the child rendered as a commodity, powerless and lacking in agency. Early childhood education is conceptualised as 'an investment in the child's entrepreneurial adult potential' (Lightfoot-Rueda, 2015: 99) and 'learning' becomes a noun: something which is acquired, rather than a process: something which is done. Important discourses of democracy, collaboration, learning needs and methods are silenced. The sociocultural status of the family is pathologised (Lucas, 2011): poor 'performance' is seen as a consequence of family deficit rather than a deficit of the education system. Severe constraints on how the child can learn are implied: there appears to be no place for the child's personal preferences, needs and interests to be engaged with, though empty phrases suggest that they are part of policy in the field.

An additional discourse of school readiness, arising from concern that some children are entering primary school 'unprepared' becomes apparent (Evans, 2015). The Department for Education has funded places for two-year-old children partly to enable practitioners in early years to enable children at risk of social skills or developmental delay to become 'school ready' (see also Ofsted's (2014) report *Are You Ready? Good Practice in School Readiness* about support for disadvantaged children starting school). There appears to be a shift in talking about two-year-olds as being at 'school' (e.g. Moylett and Grenier, 2014) rather than in nursery, kindergarten, preschool and so on. 'School' tends to be connoted with formal learning, organisation and imposed curricula, all of which are in tension with concepts of the child as a unique and agentic learner, determining the direction of her own learning in collaboration with others – parents, practitioners, or other children.

In sum, within policy documents, the two-year-old child emerges as a commodity, an object to be acted upon, but who remains silent. The child is measured, assessed and delivered to, but rarely consulted or listened to, in spite of injunctions to practitioners to do exactly that. The discourses suggest a universal concept of the child, who can be acted on in only one way: the way which 'works'. But as Biesta (2007) asks: what if 'what works' doesn't work?

Parental advice

There is a body of literature which aims to offer advice to parents who want to understand their two-year-old child and how to work with them to help them learn. Some of the literature focuses on the kinds of milestone the child might reach in their growth, whilst others focus on behaviour management, and in particular, the phase often labelled 'the terrible twos'. Cresswell (2010) traces the origin of the phrase 'terrible twos' to a film *The Terrible Twos and Trusting Threes*, issued by the Canadian Department of National Health and Welfare (Stodgill, 1950), though Kopp (1992) finds it mentioned in a 1943 paper by Gesell and Ilg. So, for at least 70 years, two-year olds have been frequently constructed in literature for parents and practitioners as troublesome, 'terrible twos', the convenient alliteration helping to inflate one characteristic of developing, pre-verbal children. Even books for small children help to perpetuate the idea that two-year-olds are troublesome: in a small illustrated story by Reich and Bracken – *Care Bears and the Terrible Twos* – '[t]he Care Bears help cheer up Melinda, who is afraid her birthday will be spoiled by the behaviour of her little brother and sister, two-year-old twins' (Reich and Bracken, 1984). The connotations of Melinda being 'afraid' and the perceived 'spoiling' behaviour of the children combine to make it appear that this phase of childhood is something to be dreaded.

Yet practitioners and parents alike will often talk about the joy of watching two-year-old children exploring and beginning to construct their worlds, and their identities within it. It can be an age of wonder and delight in discovery, as well as an age of frustration at the lack of ability to express emerging emotions and concepts. Parental advice documents are written to assist parents in the management and understanding of their children: sources include websites; leaflets available in nurseries, surgeries and schools; self-help books by academics and practitioners from a range of perspectives; and settings such as crèches, nurseries and schools. In many of these documents, the focus is on the behaviour of the two-year-old and in particular, tantrums, characterised in Gesell and Ilg's (1943) phrase 'the terrible twos', although there is some attempt to shift away from the negativity of that phrase and substitute with 'tender twos' (Ames and Ilg, 1976) or 'terrific twos' (e.g. Dukes and Smith, 2014). The important point to note is that writers tend to adopt short, pithy phrases that aim to summarise a period through which these young persons are passing: the difficulty with such phrases being that they stick, are simplistic and tend

58 Gill Boag-Munroe

to ignore the other characteristics of the phase of learning. The child is no longer a person with unique qualities, but is instead subsumed under a label, which leads parents and practitioners to deal with the child as though they are the characteristic described, rather than a complex individual. The label raises parents' and practitioners' expectations so that they are then alert to anything which appears to conform to the anticipated behaviour; or it leads them to, possibly, mistaken interpretations of what they are hearing and observing.

It is noticeable in the texts offering advice on the management of two-year-olds that the language used to discuss them is often negatively connoted. A parent searching the internet for advice on how to deal with the 'terrible twos', using that as a search term, would encounter upwards of 656,000 potential results. A search for 'two-year-old' collocated with 'tantrum' yielded 328,000 results, though not all were relevant. A final search for 'terrific twos' (a phrase currently in use in opposition to the 'terrible twos' tag) yielded 80,400 results, mostly related to titles of books and names of nurseries. Thus, on the internet at least, a two-year-old is more likely to be labelled using the negatively connoted term than by the positively connoted one, though there is an argument to suggest that both adjectives are effectively equally demeaning. Both phrases point to an age, a developmental phase, rather than to an individual child.

A reading of Dukes and Smith, (2014), and the Zero to Three website, for example, offered the descriptors represented in Table 5.1.

TABLE 5.1 Descriptors of the child drawn from parental advice documents (listed in references)

Words/phrases with positive connotations	Words/phrases with negative connotations
Persistent	Persistent
Joyful to despair	Joyful to despair
Likes to laugh	Terrible twos
Looks for fairness	Tantrums
Terrific	Tide of strong emotions
'a pleasure … but … '	Complex emotional lives
	Feelings swing wildly
	Meltdown
	Acts out
	Challenging behaviour
	Emotionally temperamental
	Stubborn
	Rigid about routines
	Demanding
	Possessive about caregivers
	Develops fears
	Can be OTT with hugging
	Cries easily
	Frustrated
	'very, very hard work' (Reid, 1992)

Talking about two-year-olds **59**

What is most noticeable about the table is the dominance of negatively connoted words, most of which are to do with emotional responses. If we are describing a child's emotional development in these negative terms, we need to ask how the child might interpret our responses, and then what they are learning about themselves as emotional beings.

Unlike in the policy documents, the child is partially visible in texts offering parental advice, albeit constructed in very limited ways. The focus is often on helping the parent to understand why 'difficult' behaviour arises, and on how the parent might manage difficult and emotional responses to interactions, which raises the possibility that readers anticipate patterns of behaviour in two-year-olds which may not actually manifest. They set up an opposition between parent and child and appear to have the aim of assisting the parent to 'tame' the child, to place parental or societal boundaries around emotions, rather than to listen to the child and work with them to manage what is happening.

Conclusion

Practitioners and parents step into and out of their figured worlds several times a day, taking discourses from one world into the next. Two-year-olds are expected to be able to make some of the shifts with them, but are only just beginning to learn the basic structures of language. There are questions to be asked about the tectonics (Curt, 1994) of the discourses: how are they interacting, fusing, confusing? Where, in all of the noise and shifting, is the practitioner's language for the child? How might the individual child be understood, or even identified, in the context of globalisation, understood as worldwide marketisation?

Such a blend of discourses points to a confused understanding of the child from the practitioner's perspective: are they a commodity to be obtained in the market, as policy documents construct them? A unique, agentic individual as some of the academic literature suggests? Or a collection of behaviours to be managed, as found in parental advice literature? Bronfenbrenner's model of the ecological context of the child shows how tiny and isolated the child can appear in the literature (see Figure 5.1). However, the mental gymnastics demanded of the practitioner in stepping in and out of these discourses is challenging, and creates potential for confusion about which role the practitioner needs to adopt at any point in her working day (Alvestad et al., 2014). Similarly, there is potential for loss of focus on the child as an individual with her own thoughts and needs, and on what practice is actually about (Jonsson and Williams, 2013).

Bronfenbrenner's model (see Figure 5.1 above) also offers perspective on how the child might be looking outwards from the centre of her learning environment. Although she does not come into direct contact with the outer circles, the people in her inner circles are influenced by those outer circles, potentially creating tension in the range of identities they offer the child through the different discourses they use in shaping the child's identity. Discourses are brought into the inner circles by the adults whom the child encounters, but how is the child to negotiate which

60 Gill Boag-Munroe

discourses are most helpful in forming their own agency? How can a two-year-old offer resistance to being identified as 'a terrible two', a commodity, or a problem to be solved? Where can the two-year-old find descriptors of herself which have more positive connotations? When the adult uses discourses which shape the child to become what the adult understands the child to be ('a terrible two'), how can the child deal with the dissonance she feels, other than by conforming to the stereotype and having a tantrum to express the frustration they feel, because they do not have the language to negotiate an alternative identity for themselves?

Finally, where the child is viewed as a commodity within a discourse of marketisation, the child becomes a tool in an activity of trading. For the two-year-old child, who wants to be seen as a person in her own right, and who wants to be able to express her feelings and needs, to be rendered little more than a tool can make her feel valued only for her usefulness, and, at times, when she is not useful, perhaps left outside the social and cultural practices she is trying so hard to become part of.

Questions

What sort of words do you/your colleagues/your children's parents/children themselves use to refer to two-year-olds? How might these be influencing two year-olds' developing identities? And how might you change this for the better?

Further reading

Brooker, L. and Woodhead, M (2008). *Developing Positive Identities: Early Childhood In Focus 3. Diversity and Young Children.* Available at: www.ecdgroup.com/docs/lib_005464256.pdf (Accessed on: 27/07/2017).

This book covers themes from this and previous chapters about the development of a positive identity in early childhood. Building on theory and evidence, different authors discuss supporting positive identity/identities, how this can be affected by adversities, social exclusion and discrimination, and how young children's resilience can be promoted.

References

Alvestad, T., Bergem, H., Eide, B., Johansson, E., Os, E., Pálmadóttir, H., Samuelsson, I.P. and Winger, N. (2014). Challenges and Dilemmas Expressed by Teachers Working in Toddler Groups in the Nordic Countries. *Early Child Development and Care*, 184(5), 671–688.

Ames, L.B. and Ilg, F.L (1976). *Your Two Year Old: Terrible or Tender.* New York: Dell.

Astington, J.W. and Edward, M.J. (2010). The Development of Theory of Mind in Early Childhood. In *Encyclopedia on Early Childhood Development*, available at: www.child-encyclopedia.com/social-cognition/according-experts/development-theory-mind-early-childhood (Accessed on: 30/11/2016).

Bakhtin, M.M. (1981). *The Dialogic Imagination: Four Essays.* (ed. Holquist, M.; trans, Emerson, G. and Holquist, M.). Austin, TX: University of Texas Press.

Biesta, G. (2007). Why "What Works" Won't Work: Evidence-Based Practice and the Democratic Deficit in Educational Research. *Educational Theory*, 57(1), 1–22.

Boag-Munroe, G. (2004). Wrestling with Words and Meanings: Finding a Tool for Analysing Language in Activity Theory. *Educational Review*, 56(2), 165–182.

Bronfenbrenner, U. (1979). *The Ecology of Human Development*. Cambridge, MA: Harvard University Press.

Cohen, L. (2009). The Heteroglossic World of Preschoolers' Pretend Play. *Contemporary Issues in Early Childhood*, 10(4), 331–342.

Cresswell, J. (2010). *Oxford Dictionary of Word Origins*. Oxford: Oxford University Press.

Curt, B.C. (1994). *Textuality and Tectonics: Troubling Social and Psychological Science*. Buckingham: Open University.

Department for Education (DfE) (2014). *Early Education and Childcare: Research Priorities and Questions*. London: DfE.

Derry, J. (2009). Vygotsky, Brandom and Psychology. *Record of Clinical-Philosophical Pedagogy*, 9, 159–162.

Dukes, C. and Smith, M. (2014). *Provision and Progress for Two-Year-Olds*. London: Sage.

Evans, K. (2015). Reconceptualizing Dominant Discourses in Early Childhood Education: Exploring 'Readiness' as an Active-Ethical-Relation. *Complicity: An International Journal of Complexity and Education*, 132(1), 32–51.

Freire, P. (1970). *Pedagogy of the Oppressed*. New York: Herder and Herder.

Gesell, A. and Ilg, F.L. (1943). *Infant and Child in the Culture of Today*. New York: Harper & Row.

Gopnik, A., Meltzoff, A.N. and Kuhl, P.K. (2001). *How Babies Think: The Science of Childhood*. London: Weidenfeld and Nicholson.

Hardman, J. (ed.) (2012). *Childhood and Adolescent Development: A South African Socio-Cultural Perspective*. Cape Town: Oxford University Press.

Holland, D., Lachiocotte, W., Skinner, D. and Cain, C. (1998). *Identity and Agency in Cultural Worlds*. Cambridge, MA: Harvard University Press.

Jonsson, A. and Williams, P. (2013). Communication with Young Children in Preschool: The Complex Matter of a Child Perspective. *Early Child Development and Care*, 183(5), 589–604.

Kopp, C.B. (1992). Emotional Distress and Control in Young Children. *New Directions for Child Development*, 55(Spring), 41–56.

Lave, J. and Wenger, E. (1991). *Situated Learning: Legitimate Peripheral Participation*. Cambridge: Cambridge University Press.

Lightfoot-Rueda, T. (2015). Human Capital Theory and Shifting Perceptions of Teachers in the United States. In Lightfoot-Rueda, T., Peach, R.L., Leask, N. (eds), *Global Perspectives on Human Capital in Early Childhood Education: Reconceptualizing Theory, Policy, and Practice*. New York: Palgrave Macmillan, 105–118.

Lucas, P.J. (2011). Some Reflections on the Rhetoric of Parenting Programmes: Evidence, Theory, and Social Policy. *Journal of Family Therapy*, 33(2), 181–198.

Moss, P. (2014). *Transformative Change and Real Utopias in Early Childhood Education: A Story of Democracy, Experimentation and Potentiality*. London: Routledge.

Moss, P. (2015). Time For More Storytelling. *European Early Childhood Education Research Journal*, 23(1), 1–4.

Moylett, H. and Grenier, J. (2014). *Including Two-year-olds in Schools: A Briefing for School Leaders*. Early Education/Nursery World. Available at: www.early-education.org.uk/including-two-year-olds-schools-briefing-school-leaders (Accessed on: 16/09/2017).

Ofsted (2014). *Are You Ready? Good Practice in School Readiness*. Available at: www.gov.uk/government/publications/are-you-ready-good-practice-in-school-readiness (Accessed on: 16/09/2017).

Reich, A. and Bracken, C. (1984). *Care Bears and the Terrible Twos*. New York: Random House Publishers.

Reid, S. (1992) *Understanding Your 2 Year Old*. London: Rosendale Press.

Rogoff, B., Mistry, J.J., Goncu, A. and Mosier, C. (1993). Guided Participation in Cultural Activity by Toddlers and Caregivers. *Monographs of the Society for Research in Child Development*, 58 (7, Serial No. 236).

Stodgill, C.G. (1950). *Terrible Twos and Trusting Threes*. Ottawa, Canada: National Film Board of Canada.

Urrieta, L. Jr. (2007). Figured Worlds and Education: An Introduction to the Special Issue. *The Urban Review*, 39(2), 107–116.

Vanderbroeck, M., Coussée, F. and Bradt, L. (2010). The Social and Political Construction of Early Childhood Education. *British Journal of Education Studies*, 58(2), 139–153.

Vygotsky, L.S. (1981). The Genesis of Higher Mental Functions. In Wertsch, J.V. (ed.), *The Concept of Activity in Soviet Psychology*. Armonk, NY: M.E. Sharpe, 144–188.

Vygotsky, L.S. (1986). *Thought and Language* (translated Kozulin, A.). Cambridge, MA: MIT Press.

Wagner, J.T. and Einarsdottir, J. (eds.) (2006). *Nordic Childhoods and Early Education: Philosophy, Research, Policy and Practice in Denmark, Finland, Iceland, Norway and Sweden*. Greenwich, CT: Information Age Publishing.

Wild, M., Silberfeld, C. and Nightingale, B. (2015). More? Great? Childcare? A Discourse Analysis of Two Recent Social Policy Documents Relating to the Care and Education of Young Children in England. *International Journal of Early Years Education*, 23(3), 230–244.

Websites

Specimen websites offering tips for dealing with tantrums and 'terrible twos' and used in developing this chapter:

> www.kidspot.com.au/parenting/toddler/toddler-behaviour/toddler-tantrums-taming-the-terrible-twos
>
> www.supernanny.co.uk/Advice/-/Parenting-Skills/-/Discipline-and-Reward/No-More-Tantrums.aspx
>
> www.parenting.com/article/toddler-temper-tantrums
>
> www.askdrsears.com/news/sears-family-blog/how-handle-2-year-olds-tantrums
>
> www.babycenter.com/0_tantrums-why-they-happen-and-how-to-handle-them_63649.bc
>
> www.mayoclinic.org/healthy-lifestyle/infant-and-toddler-health/basics/infant-and-toddler-health/hlv-20049400
>
> www.zerotothree.org/resources/326-toddlers-and-challenging-behavior-why-they-do-it-and-how-to-respond

6

WAYS OF WORKING WITH TWO-YEAR-OLDS

Jan Georgeson

Introduction

Having discussed interaction between adult and child (Chapter 2), and the discourses that are evoked or invoked in interactions (Chapter 5), in this chapter we explore how these relate to pedagogy and the development of professional quality of anticipatory watchfulness. Building on Shotter's ideas, introduced in Chapter 2, of moment-by-moment relational responding based on anticipation and awareness of the other person's needs, interests and capacities, different theoretical strands will be woven together to highlight the foundational significance for early years practitioners of relational pedagogy. I interpret relational pedagogy broadly, as a way of working both with and for children that is based on our connectivity and interconnectivity as human beings (Papatheodorou, 2009).

Discourses about two-year-olds, based on society's attitudes to children emerging from babyhood as mobile, determined, independent but volatile individuals, permeate talk, routines and the physical environment of early years settings (Chapter 5). All settings are, however, also shaped by their own histories and populated by adults with individual identities and past experiences and by children with their own short histories and developing identities. This will influence every aspect of the ways in which settings operate, and the extent to which they might develop an ethos of what has been described as 'pedagogic sensitivity' (van Manen, 2008; Nislin et al., 2016).

Practitioners find out about a setting's ethos as they take part in routine activities and interactions in the workplace. By participating in communities of practice within schools, nurseries and preschools (Lave and Wenger, 1991), practitioners learn about what is considered acceptable and appropriate from colleagues' reactions, both verbal and non-verbal, to what is said and done. They are developing the capacity for professional attention, learning about what is important to people in

64 Jan Georgeson

their setting, starting to 'notice' examples of this, and then looking out for ways to pursue this in the course of their daily work. As practitioners become more familiar with the way things work in their setting and more confident in their practice, they are likely to start to contribute more of their own ideas, based on their experiences and on theoretical understanding built up during initial and ongoing professional development. This is what Lave and Wenger (1991) describe as the process of 'legitimate peripheral participation'; new members of an organisation begin by taking part in more routine aspects of activities and then, once familiar and trusted, become engaged in gradually more complex tasks and move from the edge towards the centre. As this happens, new recruits can start to change the way things are done, by bringing in their own ideas and experiences.

I will next explain my understanding of relational pedagogy through interconnected theories of pedagogical interaction and professional identity, and then use this framework to discuss an example of practice showing adults working in different ways to support the learning and development of two-year-olds.

Relational anticipation

Like Chapter 2, this chapter is about intersubjectivity – what happens between individuals as they interact. Chapter 2 focused on the child developing an understanding of self and the world; this chapter focuses instead on practitioners and how they use their understanding of the child-in-context to support learning. In many ways, practitioners learning to work in a new early years setting undergo a similar transition to that experienced by two-year-olds as they join an early years setting for the first time, except that adults have a lot more life experience to inform their expectations of how people might act, react and interact in such a context.

Shotter (2008) argues that what we say in the course of any interaction is shaped by our anticipation of the other person's response to our contribution. This has implications for all kinds of interactions between staff and children, staff and parents, and staff and colleagues. Drawing on Polanyi's and Bakhtin's work on tacit knowledge and responsivity, Shotter encourages us to look carefully at certain 'action guiding anticipations' and 'transitory understandings' shaping our responses to other people with whom we are interacting. It is this 'anticipatory sense' of what people might be about to say or do next that underpins early years practitioners' capacity to interact sensitively with children, parents and colleagues. Shotter goes on to argue that it is not just our words which reveal this anticipatory responding; we make tiny movements, such as nodding and gesturing, to signal our attunement with what they (other people) are thinking:

> For present to us in our spontaneous bodily responsiveness to their voicing of their utterances as they unfold, are *action guiding anticipatory understandings* of what they might possibly say next.
>
> (Shotter, 2008: 161, italics in original)

Ways of working with two-year-olds **65**

This is important not only in developing children's confidence as learners, but also to consolidate their understanding of words and concepts as they interact with adults in the course of ordinary everyday events.

When early years practitioners interact with children, parents or colleagues, what is it that informs their capacity to respond in anticipation, and thereby help to shape the course of an interaction? To a certain extent, their responses are informed by concepts that practitioners have encountered in their training; studying child development will instil an awareness of what the possible next steps might be and encourage practitioners to look for 'buds' of development (Batista et al., 2006). This in turn will bias practitioners towards certain ways of responding that might make it more likely that these buds will flower. Cecilia Batista describes interactions with a child who had very limited language and little interest in communication, and how she responded to a 'bud' – a word segment from the child that had no meaning by itself but some communicative intent in context – as if it were a conversational turn and expanded it to the complete word. This is illustrated in an exchange below between adult and child, based on Silva and Batista (2007: 152):

- Adult: *I've got some toys for you!* Adult gives child a toy rabbit.
- Adult: *Look at this!*
- Child picks up the rabbit by the ear.
- Adult: *What is it?*
- Child pushes the rabbit away from her.
- Adult picks the rabbit up and places it near the child again.
- Adult: *It's a little bunny!*
- Child touches the rabbit, shouts '*Buh*' in an irritated way and pushes it away angrily.
- Adult: *Bunny, yes!* (in a tone indicating praise).

Cecilia responded to more and more 'buds' like this as sessions progressed and they started to flower, so that gradually the child began to interact with the people around her. Because Cecilia was able to watch a video recording of the session, she could reflect on and share the thinking behind her own responses in these blossoming interactions. Shotter argues, however, that for the most part these tiny instances of picking up, echoing or embellishing something from another's turn in a conversation happen automatically; we respond relationally and in anticipation of the other person's response without needing to think about it.

What we choose to respond to out of the whole array of another's words and actions is not, however, random but informed by our anticipation of what they are trying to do or say at that moment and, in the case of a pedagogical exchange, by our awareness of where they should be heading. We want the children we care for to succeed in life, to use their individual talents to become valued and fulfilled members of the community. Early years practitioners' knowledge of where children's learning should be heading is likely to be based on both formal and informal knowledge of child development, as well as on experiences of the individual interests and preferred ways of working specific to each child. Formal sources will include not only study of theorists such as Piaget and Vygotsky, but also guidance such as the Early Years Foundation Stage documents and Development Matters (Early Education, 2012; DfE, 2014). Practitioners need to maintain a fine balance between anticipation of another's responding informed by knowledge of what children are likely to want to do, and sensitively sowing the seeds (to use another horticultural metaphor) of the learning that children will need in the future. This is proleptic teaching – teaching in anticipation of competence (Brown et al., 1991) – informed by academic study but also by informal knowledge about 'the way things happen around here' picked up through participating in the work of that particular setting.

In addition to anticipatory encouragement and future-orientated shaping of learning, when and how we choose to respond is the result of professional 'attention, engagement and intelligent caring' (Arnold, 2005: 9) in pedagogical exchanges. As well as offering a grounding in the ethics of care developed through the work of theorists such as Noddings (2013), Arnold's description of intelligent caring below has clear connections with the different senses of 'minding' set out in Chapter 2:

> Care involves more than a feeling or attitude of warmth towards a person ... Intelligent caring embodies within it attention, engagement and an assessment of the consequences of care. The intelligent carer is mindful of the context in which the need for care arises, and mindful of the need to offer support which mobilises the other's coping strategies.
>
> (Arnold, 2005: 9)

There is a hint here of the tension for practitioners between wanting to foster children's learning and development of their individual talents, interests, particularities and peculiarities, and preparing them for what lies ahead, knowing how harshly difference – or not-matching-the-norm – can be treated within regulated systems of accountability as described in Chapter 4. Although there is agreement about the importance of children developing qualities of creativity and flexibility to equip them for the precarities of the future workplace, their progress is still likely to be tracked against narrow standards of achievement. Individual decisions about how to resolve this tension will be shaped by personal experience and our own sense of pedagogical purpose. This also informs the ways in which we respond to children, what we select to praise and when we decide to suggest they might try something else.

So we have our own complex set of personal resources, built up through everyday experiences in different contexts, informed by formal learning and combined with our own personal understanding of why children attend early years settings, ready to use in interactions with children to help them develop and learn.

Setting ethos

Although in England the various kinds of early years settings are part of the same Early Years Foundation Stage and are regulated and inspected by the same external agencies, they can function differently; a community preschool is subject to different constraints and affordances than a private day nursery or a Reception class in a school. To help us to look at how this influences practitioners, I have found it useful to think about settings as figured worlds. Figured worlds are part of the theory of identity formation in practice identified and developed by Holland et al. (1998). The concept is related to the idea of communities of practice mentioned above and in Chapter 5 but, while communities of practice focus on participation in the work of the setting, figured worlds are concerned with the identities of people doing these activities. Although something of an oversimplification, it can be helpful to think of communities of practice providing the stage on which 'figures' (particular characters) take part in the activity of the setting.

Early years settings are therefore figured worlds – 'socially produced and culturally constructed activities' (Holland et al., 1998: 40) – shaped by their own particular histories, where different people work together to provide education and care for young children.

> Figured worlds pre-exist us, and in being recruited to them, we participate in the inheritance, using already existing artefacts and discourses in our performances. The world of Western child-centred early years education (with its child-sized furniture, story times, snack times, creative and messy activities, construction materials, sand and water play, home corner and role play area) is an example of a figured world.
>
> (Barron, 2014: 254)

The elements making up the figured worlds of the early years setting are drawn from the familiar 'nursery treasure chest' of objects, routines and activities (Georgeson, 2009) that have been found to be useful by theorists and practitioners and appear across settings. The 'figures' in the early years setting are the practitioners, the parents and of course the children themselves, all of whom might take up particular positions. The different positions don't just include different job roles (like manager, room leader, first-aider) but they also include different 'ways of being' that one learns to recognise in a specific social context. Urrieta (2007) talks about the possible positions on offer in the context of a classroom:

> Positionality refers to the positions 'offered' to people in different figured worlds (whether that be of a 'loud student' or 'bad student' or 'successful student' or 'smart student').
>
> (Urrieta, 2007: 111)

68 Jan Georgeson

We could probably all think of similar 'types' of practitioner (or parent, or child) in early years contexts; in our study, we found practitioners described as the ones who were 'good with two-year-olds' or 'easy-going; happy to go anywhere in the setting' or 'love anything to do with craft' or 'always get on well with the parents' or 'the one who answers the questions when Ofsted come'. We could perhaps think of other possible ways of being ('only in it for the money'; 'a real clock-watcher'; 'doesn't like children but loves the paperwork') but these particular ways of being are perhaps more difficult positions to hold in early years settings. Furthermore, identities in figured worlds operate in the context of other aspects of personhood that shape identity such as class, gender and race (Barron, 2014: 255).

As a figure within a figured world then, how much 'wriggle room' do you have in the ways you think and say and do? In the theatrical analogy given earlier, how much can the characters deviate from the 'script'? An important aspect of Holland et al.'s depiction of figured worlds is the possibility of agency; identities, or ways of being, are not wholly determined by the position held but can be 'improvised'. However, to step out of and beyond your role, you are likely to be drawing on your personal resources discussed in the previous section and on your self-confidence built up through participating in the practice of the setting. This can depend on the development of professional agency, having the strength and commitment to your own set of educational values to negotiate and reconcile competing demands of values-led practice, accountability and regulation (Edwards, 2015).

Edwards goes on to point out the importance of support from the 'collective autonomy of an agentic profession' (Edwards, 2015: 783). Threats to professional autonomy for early years practitioners as they 'increasingly have to wrestle with demands for accountability, performativity and standardised approaches to their practice' have been well rehearsed (Osgood, 2006: 6), and it could be argued that there are still limitations on the extent to which early years practitioners might experience a sense of belonging to an agentic profession. Nonetheless, working in an early years setting can be understood as offering practitioners the possibility of particular ways of being, and one of those is being 'good with two-year-olds'. In our study, we asked key informants, managers and staff about the qualities needed for working with two-year-olds, which are discussed in Chapters 4 and 7. The next section offers an example of one manager's response and my own observations of practitioners being 'good with two-year-olds'.

Being 'good with two-year-olds'

The episode that sparked my thinking and led to this chapter occurred in one of the settings I visited during our two-year-olds research project. This setting, a rural day nursery offering flexible care to meet the needs of parents across a wide community, is described in more detail in Chapter 8. Here I want to concentrate on the different roles or positions – figures in the figured world of that day nursery – described by the manager during the interview. The 'figures' she talked about might easily have been described by other managers; I just happened to observe some of

Ways of working with two-year-olds **69**

her examples soon after the interview and they presented me with some contradictory thoughts – and figured worlds can be full of conflicts and contradictions (Urrieta, 2007).

We had been discussing the qualities needed to work with two-year olds and the manager drew my attention to the member of staff (let's call her Annie) who was lead practitioner in the under-threes room, describing her qualities of maturity, organisation and leadership and the example she provided to other staff working in that room. She contrasted this (non-specifically) with other staff who were less forthcoming, less likely to behave maturely, even though they were older.

I then went into the room and started my observations and Annie was indeed taking the lead in interacting with the babies and toddlers who were playing there. She kept up a constant commentary on the children's play, turning their manipulation of plastic cups, plates and food into a pretend picnic. Outside, another member of staff (I'll call her Pam) was standing near the top of the slide, as children played in the garden area. In contrast with her colleague indoors, she didn't say much and at first sight didn't seem to be doing much. Below are extracts from my observations of Annie and Pam.

Annie is sitting on a floor cushion in the babies and toddlers room with Simon (baby – newish to Nursery). They are looking at Katie's (who is two-years-old) shopping basket. Annie starts naming the contents of Katie's basket: 'Look at the sweetcorn. Here is a potato' and encourages children to feel the knobbly plastic food. 'Can you eat it? Do you like it? What colour is the sweetcorn?' Another girl (Carrie) is walking around with a doll and a phone; she stops and listens to Annie talking to Katie and the baby: 'Can you get your baby some milk? Is Carrie's baby having some milk? Is she hungry or thirsty? Does she want milk or food?' She gestures to the food when it's clear from Carrie's answers that she hasn't understood. Annie talks briefly to another member of staff about the sleeping schedule of another child, then goes back to asking another two-year-old girl (Susie) questions: 'Are you taking off your shoes?' Susie says 'teddy' and Annie expands to 'Have you got a teddy on your shoes?' Annie praises another child who has just put her shoes on the stool outside the soft play area, then turns to Susie and says 'would your baby like to come on a picnic with Simon?'

Pam is supervising outside on a hot July day. A group of children aged two years are playing near Pam, who is positioned at the top of the slide, at one end of the long thin outside area. Mike is rolling a ball down a piece of guttering placed on a slope. Cara is painting the wall with water and a fat paintbrush. Another boy (Joe) pours water from a large tray onto Cara's paintbrush from a small teapot, and Cara does some more painting. Mike and another girl (Ella) take turns rolling balls down the guttering. Mike then starts to collect all the balls and picks up Ella's ball when it reaches the bottom of the guttering. Ella calls out 'My ball'. Pam (practitioner) watches and waits a moment.

> Mike's activity has turned into ball-collecting. I wonder how will this fit with Ella's activity of rolling balls down the guttering? Pam pours water down the guttering from a cup. Ella holds out her hand for the cup and Pam gives it to her. Ella pours water down the guttering. Joe takes the cup from Ella, who calls out 'My cup!' Pam picks up a bucket and holds it out to Ella, who takes it and walks away from the slide. Pam comments to children at the water tray, who now include Ella, 'Are you making tea again?' Mike comes over and Ella holds tightly onto the cup as he tries to take it away. Mike goes back to his earlier game. Ella continues to play filling and emptying her cup in the water tray.

Annie's manager had told me about the priority which she placed on ensuring staff were well trained to support children's language development, and Annie was clearly putting into action everything she had learned on the recent courses. She used lots of new vocabulary; she asked lots of questions, and provided answers to them if children were not forthcoming. She was, as readers of Hart and Risley's (1995) study of the '30 million word gap' have been keen to recommend, bathing children in language. I could barely keep up with everything she said as I wrote down my observations. It is certainly true that recent programmes of training to increase understanding of ways to support language development have made it more likely that early years staff will be employing strategies to extend vocabulary, and move on from a routine closed questioning approach. Observing Pam immediately after Annie, however, made me realise that there are other less obvious aspects of working with two-year-olds that should be brought to the surface and talked about explicitly – if only to give practitioners like Pam the confidence to carry on working in her own quiet way.

Pam was an enabler of children's autonomy. It might not be obvious from the small snatch of activity in my observation, but the children outside were busy pursuing their own plans – perhaps they were schema or perhaps they were just momentary intentions – but Pam made sure that each individual could continue to do this without bumping into each other or getting upset because their plan was in danger of being overridden by another child pursuing their own plan. I noticed for example how, because of Pam's actions, Ella was learning how to hold on to resources and stand up to other more forceful children without the need for a big showdown and lengthy chat about how we all share here with our friends, don't we? Pam's quiet watchfulness was less obviously impressive than Annie's but it was just as skilful, informed by a deep understanding and anticipation of children's immediate needs – and just as important.

Valuing watchfulness

I got very excited as I reflected on what I had seen. Watchfulness was something different from 'observation', which distances the observer from moment-to-moment decision-making about how to respond to what is seen. Observation has become bound up with processes of assessment, in which practitioners record what they need to see to track children's progress, rather than watching in the course of responding (or not) to what children need. Observing (in itself) does not imply any action; watchfulness does. It is a kind of noticing with intention to act, while trusting children to take risks as they become accustomed to acting independently in pursuit of their own plans.

I started observing other practitioners stationed at the top of slides and noticed the same quiet watchfulness. Sometimes practitioners might chat with children as they climbed up the slide but often their contribution was a nudge here to avoid a collision at the bottom of the slide, an extra resource offered to smoothe turn-taking or to suggest a new activity. I mentioned this incident in talks about the project and people in the audience nodded in agreement, mentioning afterwards how much the word 'watchfulness' had resonated. I started to research the idea; it reminded me of 'pedagogic sensitivity' as defined by a Finnish team of researchers who have been investigating provision for children with special educational needs (see Nislin et al., 2016: 31) – and then I discovered the work of Max van Manen on pedagogical sensitivity and pedagogical tact. He had traced the concept back to the German philosopher Johann Friedrich Herbart over two hundred years ago (van Manen, 2008: 13). Van Manen's examples show how the concept of 'pedagogical tact' contains within it the awareness of when not to act as well as knowing how to act with sensitivity to children's feelings.

> Often tact involves a holding back, a passing over something, which is nevertheless experienced as influence by the student to whom the tactful action is directed. [...] Somehow, perceptiveness, insight, and feeling are instantly realized in a mode of acting that is tensed with a certain thoughtfulness or thinking attentiveness
>
> (van Manen, 2008: 15–16)

There are clear overlaps here with the anticipatory responsiveness described by Shotter, as well as parallels with the Japanese concept of *mimamoru*, translated by Hayashi as 'watchful non-intervention' (Hayashi, 2011). Experienced practitioners who have been working in Japanese early years settings for a long time have the confidence to know when to leave children to sort out their problems themselves. 'Watchful non-intervention' is deeply embedded in the cultural context of the Japanese curriculum but it is not something that features in ours. In the backwash from the performative culture of the statutory sector, it is very difficult to resist the temptation to 'perform' the good practitioner, especially if someone is observing you. Watchfulness coupled with anticipation and tact can, however, support children to learn to act agentically in the presence of others as they find their identities in the figured worlds of early years settings.

A recent keynote address by Julian Grenier echoed these ideas as he argued for 'noticing' as a more authentic approach to observation in the early years (Grenier, 2016). He also drew on the work of the education pioneers who watched children in order to understand their thinking better, to encourage them to be more autonomous and to know better about what children are really like, rather than to see where to place them on a developmental checklist. He too highlighted the difficulty practitioners might experience, because of the need to collect evidence from observations to demonstrate children's progress, in stepping away from 'doing observations' to noticing or being watchful.

Different ways of watching and responding

When we consider the skills and understandings that children are likely to be in the process of mastering across physical, cognitive and social domains, the two practitioners whom I observed in the excerpts above provide examples of different ways of being 'good with two-year-olds'. Supporting children's language development is undoubtedly an important aspect of provision for two-year-olds, because of the sudden explosion in vocabulary that we expect to occur at around this age. The message about the importance of language development has certainly been taken on board by providers of professional development and by setting managers. It is less certain, however, that other less visible (or perhaps less audible) aspects of the sensitive skilled work I observed with two-year-olds are influencing decisions about professional development in the same way. The two-year-olds funding initiative has raised the profile of work with younger children, and toddler and baby rooms, so perhaps practitioners will have more opportunities to see their ideas and ways of working inform setting policy and practice. Early years practitioners are often very skilled in responding to subtle aspects of what two-year-olds are doing. We need to start attending to this more, and to find ways of talking about it in settings and highlighting it more in professional development.

Questions

Did you recognise Annie and Pam as familiar types in the figured worlds of early years settings? Did you empathise with either of them or would you adopt a different position?

How might early years practitioners be helped to resolve the tension between caring *for* two-year-olds' immediate needs and accommodating their individual interests, and caring *about* how they will cope with what lies ahead and preparing them for the education system and beyond?

Further reading

Hayashi, A. and Tobin, J. (2015). *Teaching Embodied: Cultural Practice in Japanese Preschools*. Chicago: University of Chicago Press.

This book explores how Japanese early years teachers act – how they use their bodies, as well as gaze, gestures and words to convey meaning – and highlights the implicit and tacit aspects of teaching, showing how these are culturally embedded. Reading about teaching in another culture helps to make the familiar strange, promoting us to (re)consider the taken-for-granted in our own practice

Noddings, N. (2013). *Caring: A Relational Approach to Ethics and Moral Education, Updated.* Berkeley, CA: University of California Press.

This is a new edition of Noddings's well-known and much-referenced book in which she encourages us to think again about why we care and how we talk about caring, and not caring, arguing for a relational approach to caring and greater societal recognition of sensitivity.

References

Arnold, R. (2005). Empathic intelligence: The phenomenon of intersubjective engagement. In J-B. Song and S. O'Neill (eds.), *Enhancing Learning and Teaching: Pedagogy, Technology and Language.* Flaxton, Queensland: Post Pressed, 1–16.

Barron, I. (2014). Finding a voice: A figured worlds approach to theorising young children's identities, *Journal of Early Childhood Research* 12(3), 251–263.

Batista, C. G., Cardoso, L. M. and Santos, M. R. A. (2006). In search of 'buds' of development: Assessment procedures of impaired children, with severe learning difficulties, *Estudos de Psicolgia (Natal)* 11(3), 297–305.

Brown, A. L., Campione, J. C., Ferrara, R. A., Reeve, R. A. and Palincsar, A. S. (1991). Interactive learning and individual understanding: The case of reading and mathematics. In L. T. Landsmann (vol. ed.), *Culture, Schooling, and Psychological Development: Vol. 4. Human Development.* Norwood, NJ: Ablex Publishing Corporation, 136–170.

Department for Education (DfE) (2014). *Statutory Framework for the Early Years Foundation Stage (EYFS).* London: DfE.

Early Education (2012). *Development Matters in the Early Years Foundation Stage (EYFS).* London: Early Education.

Edwards, A. (2015). Recognising and realising teachers' professional agency, *Teachers and Teaching* 21(6), 779–784.

Georgeson, J. M. (2009). The professionalisation of the early years workforce. In S. Edwards and J. Nuttall (eds.), *Professional Learning in Early Childhood Settings.* Rotterdam: Sense, 115–130.

Grenier, J. (2016). Celebrating young children's learning in the Early Years Foundation Stage. Available at: http://juliangrenier.blogspot.co.uk/2016/12/celebrating-young-childrens-learning.html (Accessed on: 07/08/2017).

Hart, B. and Risley, T. (1995). *Meaningful Differences in the Everyday Experience of Young American Children.* Baltimore, MD: Paul H. Brookes Publishing.

Hayashi, A. (2011). The Japanese hands-off approach to curriculum guidelines for early childhood: Education as a form of cultural practice, *Asia-Pacific Journal of Research In Early Childhood Education* 5(2), 107–123.

Holland, D., Lachiocotte, W., Skinner, D. and Cain, C. (1998). *Identity and Agency in Cultural Worlds.* Cambridge, MA: Harvard University Press.

Lave, J. and Wenger, E. (1991). *Situated Learning: Legitimate Peripheral Participation.* Cambridge: Cambridge University Press.

Nislin, M. A., Sajaniemi, N. K., Sims, M., Suhonen, E., Maldonado Montero, E. F., Hirvonen, A. and Sirpa Hyttinen, S. (2016). Pedagogical work, stress regulation and work-related well-being among early childhood professionals in integrated special day-care groups, *European Journal of Special Needs Education* 31(1), 27–43.

Noddings, N. (2013). *Caring: A Relational Approach to Ethics and Moral Education, Updated.* Berkeley, CA: University of California Press.

Osgood, J. (2006). Deconstructing professionalism in early childhood education: Resisting the regulatory gaze. *Contemporary Issues in Early Childhood* 7(1), 5–14.

Papatheodorou, T. (2009). Exploring relational pedagogy. In T. Papatheodorou and J. Moyles (eds.), *Learning Together in the Early Years: Exploring Relational Pedagogy*. London: Routledge, 3–17.

Shotter, J. (2008). *Conversational Realities Revisited: Life, Language, Body and World*. Chagrin Halls, OH: Taos Institute Publications.

Silva, M. A. and Batista, C. G. (2007). Mediação semiótica: estudo de caso de uma criança cega, com alterações no desenvolvimento (Semiotic mediation: A case study of a blind child with developmental alterations), *Psicologia Reflexão e Crítica* 20(1), 141–149.

Urrieta, L. Jr. (2007). Figured worlds and education: An introduction to the special issue. *The Urban Review* 39(2), 107–116.

van Manen, M. (2008). Pedagogical sensitivity and teachers' practical knowing-in-action, *Peking University Education Review* 1, 1–23.

7

QUALIFICATIONS, KNOWLEDGE AND PREPAREDNESS FOR WORKING WITH TWO-YEAR-OLDS

Verity Campbell-Barr

Introduction

Chapter 4 demonstrated how quality of early years provision and the workforce have become inextricably linked; indeed, the early years workforce is central to quality (Urban, 2008). Members of the early years workforce shape the pedagogical environment and the experiences of the children, so their relationship to the quality of provision is somewhat inevitable. Assessments of quality often focus, however, on the qualification level of members of the workforce, so what does a qualification do to ensure quality? Do qualifications prepare people for working in early years or is the knowledge required for working with young children beyond just that obtained via training? Inevitably, the training undertaken by the early years workforce is an important facet in their preparation, so the chapter begins with an overview of the training requirements for those working with two-year-olds in England. However, Chapter 4 and wider debates (see Nutbrown, 2012) have raised questions about whether early years qualifications are fit for purpose, so later in this chapter I explore survey data collected with colleagues (Georgeson et al., 2014), to explore what enables someone who is working with two-year-olds to feel prepared for their role. I relate the findings from the survey to wider theoretical discussions on how those working in early years services come to know how to work with young children and, building on Chapter 6, the diverse ways in which an early years practitioner *knows*.

Who works with two-year-olds?

In England, two-year-olds access their early years place in a mixed-market model of provision, whereby maintained, private, voluntary and independent providers (including childminders) all provide places; children's experiences therefore vary (see Penn, 2009).

76 Verity Campbell-Barr

TABLE 7.1 Summary of minimum workforce and ratio requirements in England

Age of child	Qualifications	Ratios
Private, voluntary and independent sectors		
Under two years	Leader = Level 3,	1 to 3
	Half of all other staff Level 2	
Two years	Leader = Level 3,	1 to 4
	Half of all other staff Level 2	
Three to four years	Leader = Level 3,	1 to 8
	Half of all other staff Level 2	
Maintained sector		
Two to five years maintained nursery class	Level 6 (degree)	1 to 13 (2 to 26 where there is one teacher and one qualified assistant)
Two to five years maintained nursery school	Level 6 (degree) with QTS	1 to 10 (2 to 20 where there is one teacher and one qualified assistant)
Reception classes in schools		
Two to five years	Level 6 (degree) with QTS	Subject to infant class size legislation. 30 pupils per teacher.

Table 7.1 demonstrates that those working in the maintained sector (including reception classes) are required to hold a degree and have eligibility for Qualified Teacher Status (QTS), with associated pay and conditions. There are degrees available for those in the private, voluntary and independent (PVI) sectors that reflect both an increasing evidence base that higher qualifications are associated with higher-quality early years services (Mathers et al., 2007; Sylva et al., 2004) and the consequent history of seeking to upskill the early years workforce (Campbell-Barr, 2015; Georgeson and Payler, 2014). For example, in 2001 Foundation Degrees in Early Childhood were introduced as Level Five qualifications and in 2006 the Early Years Professional Status (EYPS) was introduced as an equivalent professional status at graduate level for the PVI sectors. Both initiatives reflected a wider programme of consolidating the range of qualifications available, whilst seeking to enhance the quality of the workforce in line with wider commitments to the quality of early years services (see Chapter 4). Initiatives under the New Labour Government (1997–2010) sought to ensure that the minimum training requirement in the PVI sectors was at Level Three, with all settings having a graduate by 2015, but this commitment was removed under the austerity measures of the Conservative-Liberal

Qualifications, knowledge and preparedness **77**

TABLE 7.2 Highest relevant qualifications held by paid staff in 2013

Level	Full daycare	Full daycare in children's centres	Sessional	Childminders
No qualification	4%	1%	6%	14%
At least Level 1	94%	96%	92%	78%
At least Level 2	93%	95%	92%	72%
At least Level 3	87%	93%	84%	66%
At least Level 5	20%	37%	18%	9%
At least Level 6	13%	30%	12%	7%

Data taken from Brind et al. (2014): Table 7.1a and c.
NB: Out of school, after school and holiday providers have been excluded. Maintained providers are also excluded as they are required to hold a Level Six qualification.

Democrat Coalition (2010–2015). Despite this, graduate-level qualifications remained available and the EYPS (Early Years Professional Status) was replaced by Early Years Initial Teacher Training; this did not, however, come with QTS and the associated pay and conditions. Thus, despite nearly 20 years of reviewing and amending early years training requirements, the sector remains a two-tier system split between the maintained and PVI sectors.

The PVI sectors (including childminders) make up the majority of those providing the funded two-year-old places (see Chapter 4 for an overview of the two-year-old places). Initially, the reliance on the PVI sectors might suggest that it is lower-qualified staff who are providing the funded places, but research from across the early years sector indicates that staff often have higher qualifications than those stipulated in minimum requirements (see Table 7.2), in line with a historic trend of staff becoming more qualified (Brind et al., 2014).

With the trend for obtaining higher qualifications, Table 7.3 demonstrates the number of settings that have access to a graduate, but also the average number of hours that they spend working with children.

The data on the early years workforce as a whole are encouraging, indicating that those who work in the early years have undertaken to increase their qualification levels, often to a level that is higher than required of them, and that those with a Level Six qualification are spending on average between 5.1 and 6 hours a day working directly with children. However, the data cover the whole early years sector and therefore do not relate directly to those working with two-year-olds. Prior to the introduction of the free entitlement for two-year-olds, there were concerns about the qualifications of staff who would work with two-year-olds, because these tend to be lower in baby/toddler rooms and, where graduates were employed, they tended not to work with babies and toddlers (Mathers et al., 2011). Further concerns include the finding that those who work with the youngest children have fewer professional development opportunities (Goouch and Powell, 2013), as well as questions about whether early years qualifications focused sufficiently on

78 Verity Campbell-Barr

TABLE 7.3 Proportion of settings having staff with a Level Six qualification and reported hours they spent with children in 2013

Type of provision	Proportion of settings to have at least one member of staff at Level Six	Mean hours per day spent working with children for staff at Level Six
Full daycare	59%	6
Full daycare in children's centres	87%	5.8
Sessional	48%	5.1
Nursery schools	100%	5.2
Primary schools with nursery and reception classes	98%	5.9
Primary schools with reception, but no nursery classes	98%	5.8

Data from Brind et al. (2014): Tables 6.18, 6.19 and 7.1.

appropriate pedagogical practice for work with under-threes (Dalli et al., 2011). Data from across Europe (European Commission/EACEA/Eurydice/Eurostat, 2014) indicate that the experiences of those working with children under three years is much more variable than those working with preschool-age children, with qualification and professional development requirements being typically lower amongst those working with the youngest children. The difference in requirements between those working with different age groups reflects a split model, whereby national governments often allocate responsibility for services for children from birth to three years and those from three years to school age between different governmental departments. Despite attempts to develop an integrated model, the legacy of the UK's split model persists in the two-tier system, as is apparent from the workforce requirements in different parts of the sector.

The inequalities inherent in a two-tier system for the early years workforce are a continued area of concern, criticism and campaigning in England and beyond. These inequalities within the early years workforce clearly need addressing, but the two-tier system also raises pertinent questions about the preparation of the early years workforce. If qualification level is a predictor of quality, is there any indication that the focus or other attributes of the training are important in predicting quality? Early et al. (2006) analysed research identifying higher levels of qualifications as being associated with higher-quality Early Childhood Education and Care (ECEC), to explore the nature of the qualifications and other features that could be contributing to the quality of ECEC. Early et al.'s analysis considered a range of variables (adult:child ratio, child poverty rates of the class, duration of the class, teachers' years of experience, wages, age, gender and ethnicity) alongside the educational level and major of those working in kindergartens in America, in relation to Early Childhood Environment Rating Scale-Revised (ECERS-R) and Classroom Assessment Scoring System (CLASS) scores and in addition to a number of child outcome measures. 'Years of education' was not associated with the quality measures, but there were higher 'Teaching and interaction' scores for those with a Bachelor's degree than those with an Associate degree. Amongst those who had a Bachelor's degree there were no significant differences between those who had majored in early childhood education or child development and those who had another education-focused qualification. Early et al. had indicated that experience and beliefs were modest predictors of classroom quality in an earlier study using the same data (citing Pianta et al., 2005).

Whilst applying findings from the US context to the UK is clearly problematic and the use of standardised measures reflects modernist approaches to assessing quality and child development as explored in the previous chapter, the findings do raise questions about how those working in the early years are prepared for their role. The lack of a significant difference between the types of degree means that the concerns over qualifications having a sufficient focus on two-year-old development may be misplaced. Equally, the study demonstrates that it is not solely qualifications that contribute to the preparation of the workforce, as experience and beliefs are also important.

Exploring workforce preparation

Given questions about who was working with two-year-olds, their qualification level and professional development opportunities, alongside queries about how a person comes to know how to work in the early years, a survey was undertaken as part of our project to explore the self-reported preparedness of the early years workforce, particularly those working with two-year-olds. The design of the survey was led by Sandra Mathers (who also carried out the analysis for the project report) and was based on the findings from earlier stages of the research in which key informants had raised a number of areas that were pertinent for working with two-year-olds (see Chapter 4). The survey was also supplemented by case studies within settings that included interviews with staff and observations of daily practice (see Chapter 8). The survey was administered online, with the support of local authorities and early years charities, generating 688 responses from participants who had 'agreed to take part' in the anonymous survey having read an ethics statement providing details on the aims of the research, anonymity and the use of the data. In some instances, respondents did not answer all questions; therefore, the number of responses for each question is indicated in the presentation of the data.[1] The presentation of the data begins with an overview of the participants before considering their preparedness and the variables that may have influenced this. Whilst the questions on preparedness considered working with children from birth to five years, working with children with additional needs, supporting families, multi-professional working and completing the two-year-old check, I will primarily focus on the responses relating to working with two-year-olds.

80 Verity Campbell-Barr

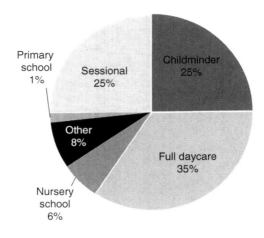

FIGURE 7.1 Settings where respondents worked

Participants

Figures 7.1 and 7.2 present the settings and sectors where the respondents worked, reflecting the reliance on the PVI sectors for the provision of the two-year-old places and early years services more generally. The average total number of places was 38.9,[2] but for those who reported the number of funded two-year-old places (N = 543), the average was 4.6. The implication is that funded two-year-olds accounted for a small proportion of the overall number of children within a setting. However, in the free text responses connected to this question, some practitioners indicated that their intention was to start offering funded places in the following term (and so offered no places at the time of completing the survey), whilst childminders noted the restrictions on the number of children they could take. The high number of childminders in the sample, along with those not yet offering places, could be distorting the reported average number of funded two-year-olds in early years settings. The indication that some settings were only at the planning stages of taking funded two-year-olds was evident in the case studies (see Georgeson et al., 2014). Therefore, it is anticipated that both the average number of funded two-year-olds in a setting and the overall number of settings providing places is likely to increase (which would be in line with government proposals). The majority of providers reported that they had previously admitted two-year-olds (72.8%) and 47.1% of respondents had previously worked directly with this age group, indicating that whilst some settings might have a history of provision for two-year-olds, individuals did not necessarily have experience of working with two-year-olds, something that is considered in more detail later in the chapter.

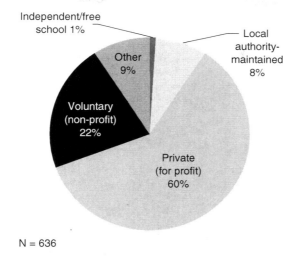

FIGURE 7.2 Sectors where respondents worked

Overall, the sample is drawn from high-quality settings, with 27.1% receiving Outstanding in their last Ofsted inspection, 62.7% Good, 9.6% Satisfactory or Requires Improvement and the remaining 0.6% Inadequate. The high-quality grades were expected as settings with Outstanding and Good grades were targeted to draw down the funding to offer the two-year-old places. Whilst some areas broadened the quality criteria in order to ensure sufficiency of places, readers should consider throughout the chapter that on the whole I am discussing settings that are of a high standard (within the constraints of the potential limitations of Ofsted as quality criteria as considered in Chapter 4).

The national trend for practitioners to complete higher levels of training than those stated in the minimum requirements (Brind et al., 2014) was evident in the survey respondents (Table 7.4) and encouragingly graduates also reported working with two-year-olds.

Overall, the survey participants were experienced, with 72% having more than ten years' experience (Table 7.5). What is encouraging for the two-year-olds accessing the free places is that just over half of respondents indicated having more than ten years' experience of working with two-year-olds, displacing concerns that it is younger and less experienced members of staff who tend to work with younger children.

The overall picture of the free early years places for two-year-olds from our survey suggests that the settings are high-quality (in consideration of the Ofsted grade), with well-qualified and experienced staff working with two-year-olds. There is the possibility that staff from the settings that are of a higher standard are more likely to be motivated to respond to an online survey and the quality requirements for which settings could offer the two-year-olds places meant that the sample would

82 Verity Campbell-Barr

TABLE 7.4 Qualification levels of respondents

Qualification	Respondents who held stated qualification	Respondents working with two-year-olds who held stated qualification
I do not hold a childcare-related qualification	3.7%	1.7%
Level 1	0.2%	0.3%
Level 2	1.1%	1.1%
Level 3	33.3%	40.3%
Level 4	12.5%	11.6%
Level 5	9.6%	10.5%
Level 6	25.6%	25.3%
Level 7 or 8	12.7%	8.2%
Other (e.g. overseas qualification)	1.3%	0.9%
	N = 543	N = 352

TABLE 7.5 Respondents' years of experience

Experience working with 0- to five-year-olds	No.	%	Experience working with two-year-olds	No.	%
Less than a year	5	0.9	Less than a year	14	2.6
One to two years	9	1.7	One to two years	23	4.3
Two to four years	38	7.0	Two to four years	77	14.3
Five to ten years	100	18.4	Five to ten years	135	25.0
Ten or more years	391	72.0	Ten or more years	290	53.8

always be skewed towards higher-quality settings. The survey was not, however, designed to be representative; instead it was intended to offer a picture of who was providing the two-year-olds places. Taking into account the quality, training and experience of the sample, I now analyse the extent to which the respondents felt prepared for offering the funded two-year-old places.

Preparedness

Interviews with key informants (see Chapter 4) indicated that offering the funded two-year-old places was not just about working with the two-year-olds, but also about working with families and other professionals. Further, prompted by concerns about the adequacy of qualifications, the questionnaire focused on how well respondents felt their qualifications had prepared them for working with children aged from birth to five years, with two-year-olds specifically, and for other aspects of

Qualifications, knowledge and preparedness

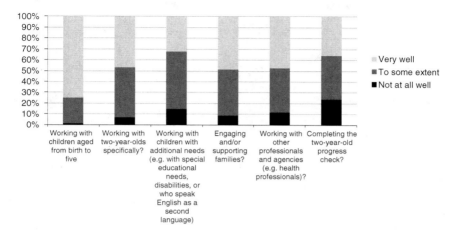

Response rates: Working with children aged from birth to five, N = 509; Working with two-year-olds specifically? N = 515; Working with children with additional needs (e.g. with special educational needs, disabilities, or who speak English as a second language) N = 511; Engaging and/or supporting families? N = 515; Working with other professionals and agencies (e.g. health professionals)? N = 516; Completing the two-year-old progress check? N = 507.

FIGURE 7.3 Respondent ratings on qualifications and preparedness

provision, such as working with families, multi-professional working and supporting children with special educational needs. Figure 7.3 demonstrates that overall, participants felt that their initial qualifications had prepared them 'very well' for working with children from birth to five years of age; however, the levels of preparedness declined when the items identified by the key informants as specific to delivering the early years places for two-year-olds were considered.

Respondents were also asked how confident they felt about related categories (see Figure 7.4). The confidence levels offer a similar pattern to those on preparedness, but indicate that confidence develops outside of initial training. However, in light of the earlier questions raised about initial training, the remaining analysis focuses on the question of preparedness and explores associated variables.

In view of the concerns about whether qualifications were fit for purpose and that training may not have always focused on this age group, I consider preparedness for working with two-year-olds in relation to qualifications and years of experience. Grouping qualifications into three categories of none to Level Three; Level Four and Five; and Level Six and higher (Figure 7.5), there is little difference in self-reported preparedness. Given the research evidence of associations between higher qualifications and quality, it was anticipated that those with a Level Six or higher qualification would report greater levels of preparedness. Whilst it is possible that those with lower qualifications might overstate their preparedness, it would seem unfair to challenge self-reported preparedness in the absence of applying an actual preparedness assessment. It may also be that those at Level Six under-report their preparedness. Key informant interviews indicated that a feature of Level Six

84 Verity Campbell-Barr

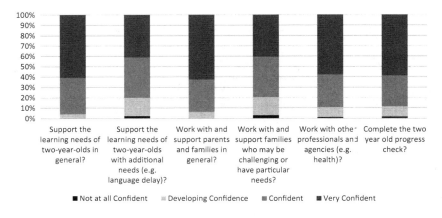

Response rates: Support the learning needs of two-year-olds in general? N = 507; Support the learning needs of two-year-olds with additional needs (e.g. language delay)? N = 508; Work with and support parents and families in general? N = 506; Work with and support families who may be challenging or have particular needs? N = 508; Work with other professionals and agencies (e.g. health)? N = 506; Complete the two year old progress check? N = 503.

FIGURE 7.4 Self-reported confidence levels

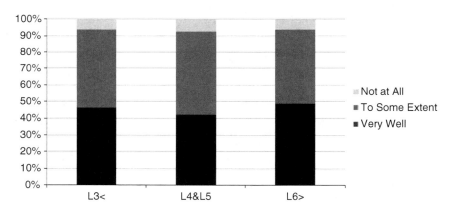

Response rates: Level Three and under, N = 208; Level Four or Five, N = 117; Level Six and over, N = 201.

FIGURE 7.5 Preparedness for working with two-year-olds in relation to qualifications

qualifications was the development of reflective practice skills that included critically evaluating practice (Georgeson et al., 2014). Therefore, it might be that those with higher qualifications are more reflective (and perhaps critical) of their level of preparedness, although this would need to be researched in more detail.

Although we were surprised that there was no indication that a higher-level qualification led to greater self-reported preparedness, the initial discussion in this chapter also questioned whether the nature of graduate qualifications could make a difference, particularly as teaching qualifications with QTS do not typically include a focus on two-year-olds, whilst EYPS covered the birth to five years age range. Considering those with QTS who responded to the question of feeling prepared to work with two-year-olds (N = 36), 58.3% reported feeling Very Well prepared and 36.1% To Some Extent. Amongst those with EYPS who responded to the same question (N = 123), 83.7% reported feeling Very Well prepared and 15.4% To Some Extent. Whilst initially this comparison appears to demonstrate that those with EYPS reported feeling more prepared, the very small numbers of respondents with QTS means that the figures should be treated with caution and indicate an area that requires further exploration.

The sector that the respondents were from was also considered in relation to their self-reported preparedness for working with two-year-olds. Amongst childminders who responded to the question (N = 137), 44.5% reported being Very Well prepared and 48.9% To Some Extent. For Full daycare (N = 181), 44.2% reported being Very Well prepared and 51.4% To Some Extent, and for Nursery Schools (N = 29) 37.9% reported being Very Well prepared and 55.2% to Some Extent (the remaining respondents indicated that they felt Not At All prepared). The small sample sizes again indicate a need to treat the data with caution, but the suggestion is that there is little difference in self-reported preparedness between sectors, which would displace earlier concerns around the mixed-market model for the implementation of the two-year-old places.

Given that qualifications and sector did not appear to be a predictor of preparedness, years of experience were also considered. Overall, respondents reported high levels of experience, so those with less than a year, one to two years and two to four years of experience were treated as one group to enable a larger group size for comparison. Figure 7.6 indicates that greater experience was associated with greater self-reported preparedness for working with two-year-olds.

Training and experience

There has been a global trend to focus on the training of the early years workforce due to the increased evidence demonstrating that training is central to quality. Whilst there are many debates that consider what quality is (see Chapter 4), there are also questions about what a qualification 'does' to improve quality. The data presented in this chapter suggest that qualifications are not a predictor of self-reported preparedness. Whilst self-reported preparedness is not the same as quality and the self-assessment is potentially problematic, questions arise as to how members of the workforce come to 'know' about and feel prepared for working in early years services. The data indicate that experience is positively related to self-reported preparedness, but this should not be read as experience being the only contributor to preparing the early years workforce. Experience is important for informing and shaping the knowledge base of those who work in early years services and whilst I aim to demonstrate how experience is a deeply embedded attribute of the early

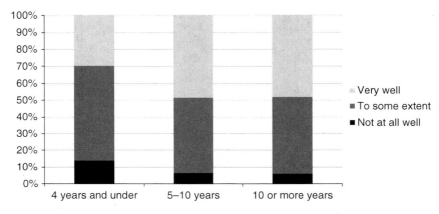

Response rates: 4 years and under, N = 52; 5–10 years, N = 100; 10 or more years, N = 391.

FIGURE 7.6 Preparedness for working with two-year-olds in relation to years of experience working with 0–5-year-olds

years workforce, I will also demonstrate that experience alone is not sufficient for working with young children.

Models of training for the early years workforce in England have traditionally been ones of apprenticeship, where there is an emphasis on the learning that takes place through working directly in early years settings (Georgeson, 2009; Payler and Locke, 2013). The NVQ (National Vocational Qualifications) model that developed in England reflected the emphasis placed on practice as students would work towards gaining their qualification (Levels Two, Three and Four) through an apprenticeship, assessed through observations and portfolios. The apprenticeship model highlights how experience is a built-in feature of early years workforce training. However, there are criticisms of the NVQ training. For example, key informants questioned whether training was fit for purpose, including questioning the skills of the assessors and the number of observations that were made of students (Georgeson et al., 2014). Other criticisms of the NVQ model have focused on how the adoption of a competence-based model leads training to focus on technocratic efficiency and 'doing things right' rather than 'doing the right things' (Vandenbroeck et al., 2013), representing wider concerns of early years training being about the person who can apply the right techniques at the right time to achieve the culturally desirable outcomes (Dahlberg and Moss, 2005).

The challenges to the training of the early years workforce should be set against two important contextual features. The first relates specifically to England where training has been through a process of review and reform for nearly 20 years, as outlined at the start of the chapter. Importantly, at the time of the research, NVQ qualifications had been reviewed and adapted, resulting in the required Level Three qualification becoming the Early Years Educator (National College for

Teaching and Leadership, 2013). Since then, proposed increased entry requirements based on GCSEs in English and Maths have been rejected in response to pressure from the sector (Nursery World, 2017). The questioning of the entry requirements and general concern with getting early years workforce training 'right' reflect broader debates on who and what is informing understandings of early years workforce training. The technocratic model serves the needs of policy objectives, particularly those in relation to supporting child development, but has been imposed on those working in the early years, rather than coming from within the sector (Campbell-Barr, 2015). Thus, the self-reported confidence in relation to training should be set against a backdrop of critiquing early years training, and this could have potentially clouded respondents' judgements of the adequacy of their training.

The practical aspects of early years training are related to a broader conception of experience as important in preparing the future workforce. This is more than experience gained whilst training, as I would argue that experience is a deeply engrained attribute of what is regarded as a 'good' member of the workforce, incorporating experience developed prior to, whilst undertaking and once working in early years services. Prior experiences include those of caring for others, such as siblings or even one's own children; those choosing to work in early years services often emphasise their prior experiences, with practical knowledge being highly valued. Working with young children is regarded as something they can 'do' as a result of these experiences (Skeggs, 1997; Penn, 2011; Vincent and Braun, 2011), but experiences whilst training or once in work can also challenge the feeling of being able to 'do' working in the early years, as practitioners find themselves negotiating the daily experiences of working with young children (Colley, 2006). Experiences (both the challenges and the rewards) are central to the continuing preparation of the early years workforce, providing a rich and varied resource to be drawn upon in future practice.

Experience is an established feature of early years workforce preparation, both through the emphasis placed on the importance of experiences by members of the workforce and through training models that combine taught elements of training with time in practice. The combination of taught and practical content reflects a coming together of theory and practice, whereby neither theory nor practice on their own is sufficient for preparing the workforce. Experience is necessary for expertise, but does not guarantee it (Ward et al., 2013), but knowledge is not merely recalling theory, as it has to be applied in order to demonstrate professional knowledge (Winch, 2014). The optimum balance between taught and practical aspects of workforce training is hard to determine, as is demonstrated by the variations that can be found between courses delivered in different countries, as well as those within the same country. Georgeson and Payler (2014) explore developments in early years workforce training in England and the balance between theory and practice and conclude that vocational routes (such as NVQs) can leave students feeling they lack the knowledge of how to respond to a particular situation, whilst theory encountered on academic routes can seem abstract when not related to

88 Verity Campbell-Barr

practice. The constant changes in training requirements in England demonstrate the continued search by policy-makers for the best way to prepare the early years workforce whilst balancing this against other agendas, such as widening participation in post-compulsory education. Thus, whilst the combination of theory and practice is important, knowing how to combine them remains an unresolved problem for early years workforce preparation.

Knowledges

Initial training is recognised as the first stage in the preparation of the early years workforce. Professional development opportunities also form an important part of shaping and developing the knowledge and skills of those who work in early years services, as well as experiences gained through daily practice. Experiences in daily practice act as a bank of knowledge, from knowing about the daily routines of working in a daycare setting, to supporting a child with toilet training and to more challenging circumstances that can be encountered when working with a child that is a witness to domestic violence. Daily experiences form 'know-how' that can be stored in the knowledge bank for use at another time, but importantly there are two aspects to 'know-how', one of knowing how to 'do' daily practice and the second of evaluating this knowledge in order to consider whether the knowing how with one child is appropriate with another child or in another setting (see Winch, 2014). Thus, those working in early years services are not just collating a bank of experiences that they can draw upon in their daily practice; they are also evaluating and combining them in order to gain the most from this rich pool of knowledge.

The difficulty is that such experience is often not articulated; it remains a tacit form of knowledge. Yet despite its tacit nature, experience is an important aspect in the ongoing preparation of early years practitioners. Katz (1972) discussed the developmental stages that those working in the early years go through in becoming 'preschool teachers'. The early years sector often focuses on child development, but members of the workforce will also have their own stages of development that have many parallels with those of a child (see Chapter 2 and 3). Katz explores how after initial training, 'teachers' (the term she uses) go through Survival — can I get through the day in one piece?; Consolidation — confirming the gains made in the first year of teaching; Renewal — asking about new developments in the field; and Maturity — coming to terms with oneself as a teacher and asking more philosophical questions of their practice. Katz's model could be treated as illustrative of the findings in our survey data, whereby those who are less experienced feel less prepared as they are at the Survival or Consolidation stage of their professional life. Katz's model is individualised, potentially fitting the experience of an individual teacher (or a childminder), but not reflecting the staff team of the PVI sectors.

Lave and Wenger's (1991) Communities of Practice model envisions learning as a social process in which a group of people share their ideas and thinking (see also Chapters 5 and 6). Members of the community build up a repertoire of shared resources that can inform daily practice, but the resources are not just about technical practice, instead being based on shared ideas of how to approach practice. Those undertaking their initial training would be on the periphery of participating in the community, but over time they will move to the centre as a result of learning through mutual engagement in shared practice. Lave and Wenger's model is more collaborative than that of Katz, demonstrating how practitioners are both informed by and inform the community of practice, whilst again drawing attention to the experience of being in practice as an important attribute of preparedness. Chapter 9 demonstrates that it is not enough to assume that practitioners move towards the centre, as it is possible that some members of the community become marginalised, with previous research acting as a warning of how those working with younger children can often seem less valued than those working with older children (Goouch and Powell, 2013). However, the centrality of experience demonstrates that becoming an early years practitioner is not an end goal to be reached, but a continuing process.

Importantly, working with disadvantaged two-year-olds as a result of the funded places highlights a range of challenging experiences that can be encountered:

> *When you think about the community we are working in, we now get [Name of Call], a call which means the police have been at the house and there has been some domestic violence thing. That's only the top of the scale but I'd say on low levels you've got children dealing with things at home that are troubling or difficult or also with their additional needs. We have quite a few children who we're not saying that they haven't been diagnosed, but probably have behaviours that might be on the autism spectrum so therefore we need a specialised response to how to settle those children in and how to enable them to link with peers in a reasonably productive way ... We are quite lucky as the parents are quite open, once they get to know us they'll come in and say, I might be losing my job or I'm struggling with mental health and then you can realise why this child is behaving in that specific manner. You know what's happening in the family so you are aware of the context ... Karen[3] often notices that, she'll set up a meeting with the parent and key worker and quite often that's the beginning, especially with the funded two-year-olds, of the story. They [parents] don't always tell their story at the beginning, Karen has to use a lot of skill so that they are not really worried about this fact, or that a little bit of support is needed, but in a gentle way. Because basically you've got a skill as a practitioner. Karen sometimes knows when they [parents] are being showed around, she knows that that child is going to be added to her list of observations and needs. These [the staff] are people that have been looking at children for years.*

The quote above from Karen's manager not only highlights the challenges that can be faced in daily practice by those providing the funded places for two-year-olds, but also the importance of experience for working with the children *and* their families.

Conclusion

Experience is central to know-how and contributes to the continuing preparedness of the workforce, and whilst I believe there is a need to articulate experience as a form of knowledge, experience alone does not create an expert. Working with young children requires different knowledge – or knowledges. In accepting knowledge in the plural, it is possible to recognise the importance of the rich and varied ways in which members of the early years workforce come to 'know' how to work with young children and that knowing is not an end goal to be reached, but a continued process of preparedness.

Questions

What knowledges do you think are important for working with young children? Where and how do you develop these knowledges?

Notes

1 The response rates presented in this chapter differ to those presented in the initial report (Georgeson et al., 2014), as in the initial report only those who had answered all questions were included.
2 This figure does not include two outliers, where respondents reported offering 900 and 1219 places.
3 The name has been changed to ensure anonymity.

Further reading

Campbell-Barr, V. (forthcoming). The silencing of the knowledge-base in early childhood education and care professionalism. *International Journal of Early Years Education*, accepted August 2017.

The concept of knowledges for working in early childhood education and care and the combination of know-that and know-how is explored in depth within this paper, set against the context of an interest in the 'quality' of services.

Georgeson, J., and Payler, J. (2014). Qualifications and quality in the early years foundation stage, in J. Moyles, J. Payler, and J. Georgeson (eds.), *Early Years Foundations*. Maidenhead: McGraw Hill Education, 52–64.

This chapter provides a comprehensive overview of the changes and related debates that have taken place around early years qualifications in the English context.

References

Brind, R., McGinigal, S., Lewis, J., Ghezelayagh, S., Ransom, H., Robson, J., Street, C., and Renton, Z. (2014). *Childcare and Early Years Providers Survey 2013: TNS BMRB Report JN 117328*. London: DfE.

Campbell-Barr, V. (2015). The research, policy and practice triangle in early childhood education and care, in R. Parker-Rees and C. Leeson (eds.), *Early Childhood Studies*. Exeter: Learning Matters, 234–248.

Colley, H. (2006). Learning to labour with feeling: Class, gender and emotion in childcare education and training. *Contemporary Issues in Early Childhood*, 7(1), 15–29.

Dahlberg, G., and Moss, P. (2005). *Ethics and Politics in Early Childhood Education*. London: Routledge/Falmer.

Dalli, C., White, E. J., Rockel, J., Duhn, I., Buchanan, E., Davidson, S., Ganly, S., Kus, L., and Wang, B. (2011). Quality early childhood education for under-two-year-olds: What should it look like? A literature review. *Report to the Ministry of Education*. New Zealand: Ministry of Education. www.educationcounts.govt.nz/__data/assets/pdf_file/0009/89532/965_QualityECE_Web-22032011.pdf. (Accessed on: 09/08/2017).

Early, D. M., Bryant, D. M., Pianta, R. C., Clifford, R. M., Burchinal, M. R., Ritchie, S., Howes, C., and Barbarin, O. (2006). Are teachers' education, major, and credentials related to classroom quality and children's academic gains in pre-kindergarten? *Early Childhood Research Quarterly*, 21(2), 174–195.

European Commission/EACEA/Eurydice/Eurostat (2014). *Key Data on Early Childhood Education and Care in Europe 2014 Edition*. Luxembourg: Publications Office of the European Union.

Georgeson, J. M. (2009). The professionalisation of the early years workforce. In S. Edwards and J. Nuttall (eds.), *Professional Learning in Early Childhood Settings*. Rotterdam: Sense, 115–130.

Georgeson, J., Campbell-Barr, V., Boag-Munroe, G., Mathers, S., Caruso, F., and Parker-Rees, R. (2014). *Two-year-olds in England: An Exploratory Study*. London: TACTYC.

Georgeson, J., and Payler, J. (2014). Qualifications and quality in the early years foundation stage, in J. Moyles, J. Payler, and J. Georgeson (eds.), *Early Years Foundations*. Maidenhead: McGraw Hill Education, 52–63.

Goouch, K., and Powell, S. (2013). Orchestrating professional development for baby room practitioners: Raising the stakes in new dialogic encounters. *Journal of Early Childhood Research*, 11(1), 78–92.

Katz, L. (1972). Developmental stages of preschool teachers. *The Elementary School Journal*, 73(1), 50–54.

Lave, J., and Wenger, E. (1991). *Situated Learning: Legitimate Peripheral Participation*. Cambridge: Cambridge University Press.

Mathers, S., Ranns, H., Karemaker, A., Moody, A., Sylva, K., Graham, J., and Siraj-Blatchford, I. (2011). Evaluation of the graduate leader fund. *Report to the UK Department of Education*, DFE-RR144, London: Department for Education.

Mathers, S., Sylva, K., Joshi, H., Hansen, K., Plewis, I., Johnson, J., George, A., Linskey, F., and Grabbe, Y. (2007). *Quality of Childcare Settings in the Millennium Cohort Study*. London: Department for Education and Skills.

National College for Teaching and Leadership (2013). *Early Years Educator (Level 3): Qualifications Criteria*. London: NCTL.

Nursery World (2017). GCSE Level 3 rules scrapped as Early Years Workforce Strategy is released, 3 March . 2017. www.nurseryworld.co.uk/nursery-world/news/1160488/gcse-level-3-rules-scrapped-as-early-years-workforce-strategy-is-released. (Accessed on: 08/08/2017)

Nutbrown, C. (2012). *Foundations for Quality: The Independent Review of Early Education and Childcare Qualifications. Final Report*, DFE-00068-2012, London: Department for Education.

Payler, J. K., and Locke, R. (2013). Disrupting communities of practice? How 'reluctant' practitioners view early years workforce reform in England. *European Early Childhood Education Research Journal*, 21(1), 125–137.

Penn, H. (2009). International perspectives on quality in mixed economies of childcare. *National Institute Economic Review*, 207(1), 83–89.

Penn, H. (2011). *Quality in Early Childhood Services.* Maidenhead: McGraw Hill.

Pianta, R., Howes, C., Burchinal, M., Bryant, D., Clifford, R. M., Early, D. M., and Barbarin, O. (2005). Features of pre-kindergarten programs, classrooms, and teachers: Prediction of observed classroom quality and teacher–child interactions. *Applied Developmental Science*, 9(3), 144–159.

Skeggs, B. (1997). *Formations of Class & Gender: Becoming Respectable.* London: Sage.

Sylva, K., Melhuish, E., Sammons, P., Siraj-Blatchford, I., and Taggart, B. (2004). *The Effective Provision of Pre-school Education (EPPE) Project.* Final Report: A Longitudinal Study Funded by the DfES 1997–2004. London: Institute of Education, University of London/Department for Education and Skills/Sure Start (Accessed on: 08/08/2017).

Urban, M. (2008). Dealing with uncertainty: Challenges and possibilities for the early childhood profession. *European Early Childhood Education Research Journal*, 16(2), 135–152.

Vandenbroeck, M., Peeters, J., and Bouverne-De Bie, M. (2013). Lifelong learning and the counter/professionalisation of childcare: A case study of local hybridizations of global European discourses. *European Early Childhood Education Research Journal*, 21(1), 109–124.

Vincent, C., and Braun, A. (2011). 'I think a lot of it is common sense ...' Early years students, professionalism and the development of a 'vocational habitus'. *Journal of Education Policy*, 26(6), 771–785.

Ward, L., Grudnoff, L., Brooker, B., and Simpson, M. (2013). Teacher preparation to proficiency and beyond: Exploring the landscape. *Asia Pacific Journal of Education*, 33(1), 68–80.

Winch, C. (2014). Know-how and knowledge in the professional curriculum, in M. Young and J. Muller (eds.), *Knowledge, Expertise and the Professions.* London: Routledge, 47–60.

8

DIFFERENT PLACES FOR TWO-YEAR-OLDS

Jan Georgeson

Introduction

The earlier chapters of this book have referred briefly to some of the contexts in which we carried out the research – the places for two-year-olds to which we were directed by Key Informants as examples of how the two-year-olds offer was playing out in their context. Just as reliance by the English early years and childcare system on a mixed-market model (Penn, 2009) shapes who is working with two-year-olds (see Chapter 7), the range of providers we encountered also reflects the consequent complexity. The two-year-olds initiative funded places with different kinds of providers, and in our study we visited a childminder, community preschools, day nurseries, children's centres and schools (Georgeson et al., 2014). The settings included variations within the main categories of private, voluntary, independent and maintained provision; some settings were part of a chain, or a playgroup on a school site or daycare attached to a children's centre. We talked to managers about their provision for two-year-olds and in six settings we were also able to carry out observations and talk to staff about what we had noticed.

Table 8.1 provides a summary of the early years providers visited (or, in the case of setting 11, contacted by telephone), showing the nature of their provision in general and their response to the two-year-olds offer. The 11 settings had different histories and had been set up for different purposes, and not surprisingly they had different approaches to offering provision for two-year-olds. The settings varied in the amount of previous experience which they had had in working with two-year-olds, the support structures they were able to access, the structure of the sessions and their understanding of the purpose of early years provision in general and the funded offer in particular. In effect, the settings were different figured worlds (Holland et al., 1998) in which children, parents and practitioners were positioned differently. In the sections that follow, overviews from four case study settings (all

TABLE 8.1 Summary of settings

	Setting details	Two-year-old offer	Overall provision	Area
1★	Community preschool	19 funded two-year-olds (21 in total). Previously only 2 two-year-olds.	Two years to five years. Registered for 30 a session, 75 on roll.	City, Southern England
2	Children's centre	25 funded places. History of taking two-year-olds.	Three months to five years. 36 registered places. 57 on roll.	City, Southern England
3★	Small private daycare chain, attached to children's centre	10 funded places. Demand for more places, but no capacity. History of taking two-year-olds.	Three months to five years.	City, Southern England
4★	Primary school with a Foundation Stage unit	Eight funded places. Encouraged by LA to take two-year-olds as had started to take rising threes.	55 on roll. Currently offer three- and four-year-old early education places.	City, Southern England
5★	Rural daycare	Five funded places. Can take up to 13. Children on waiting list for September.	Registered for 29 per session, 81 on roll. 0 months to 11yrs.	Large county, rural areas, Southern England
6	Primary school planning provision	20 two-year-olds, 18 places taken for September 2014.	Currently offer three- and four-year-old early education places.	Large county, rural areas, Southern England
7★	Childminder	2 two-year-olds (originally not entitled to place but later given vouchers).	Up to six children (depending on ages).	Large county, rural areas, Southern England
8	Not-for-profit playgroup on school site with children's centre	Offer 12 places, morning only. Moving to 16 mornings and 16 afternoons in September 2014.	116 registered places	Small county, Northern England
9	Private nursery (limited company status)	Nine taking up offer, feels some parents are not using it.	0 months to 11 years. (Playgroup up to three years. Three+ in school.)	Small county, Northern England

Different places for two-year-olds **95**

TABLE 8.1 (*Cont.*)

	Setting details	Two-year-old offer	Overall provision	Area
10★	Small private daycare chain	Established to meet shortfall in places. As a chain have a history of taking two-year-olds. 52 funded children on roll.	Three months to five years full daycare. 66 registered places.	London
11	Independent daycare provider	22 places for two-year-olds (approx. 15 funded). History of taking two-year-olds.	Three months to five years. 68 places for under threes.	London

Starred settings (★) are those where observations were carried out in addition to interviews with the manager.

names are pseudonyms) give a glimpse into these figured worlds and the different experiences of the two-year-olds who found themselves there.

A childminder

Context

Hilary was looking after two two-year-olds on the day I visited as well as her own children, a girl and boy aged five and three. They lived in a bungalow on the edge of a rural hamlet and the children spent their time between the open-plan kitchen-diner-living room, enclosed garden and adjacent field. Hilary also told me about taking children out for day trips to woods, beaches and places of interest, as well as walks to local parks, aiming for at least one outing and one 'at home' day for each child each week. The children had easy access to a changing range of toys each day, and also met up with the child-friendly dog, two rabbits and a pond full of Koi fish. Observation during the session showed that interactions between Hilary and the children in her care were finely tuned (in terms of sentence length, complexity of syntax and vocabulary) to the children's different ages and, perhaps unsurprisingly, had a natural quality arising as they did in the course of domestic events and familiar play routines.

Hilary held a NVQ Level 3 qualification and had previously worked in nurseries. Childminding was fitting in well with caring for her own children at the time and she hoped to study further once her own children were at school. Hilary was able to keep up-to-date through the affordable training on offer, which took place in the early evening, perfect for a childminder, within 20 minutes' travel time from home. Hilary attended PACEY (Professional Association for Childcare and Early Years) meetings once a month, where she found it useful to talk about practice and behaviour issues with other childminders.

Hilary liaised frequently with the local preschool and primary school, as some children split their time between childminder and preschool; 'learning journey' documents were therefore shared. Hilary worked closely with parents to support children's development, offering advice 'mum-to mum'. She thought, however, that she would find this harder if she didn't 'click' with a parent; minded children and their parents became 'part of the family' and parents stayed friends after the childminding arrangement ended.

Approach to provision for two-year-olds

Hilary saw the funded two-year-olds initiative as offering support for families on lower incomes, to avoid the possibility of children who might 'slip through the net' and arrive at school without basic skills. She added that the two-year-olds offer meant that problems could be picked up earlier and children could be given 'a bit of a boost' before they became eligible for three-year-olds funding at a 'crucial development stage'; this idea of the funded places providing a 'pre-preschool' was mentioned in other settings in the study too.

Hilary told me she tried to look at things 'through a child's eye, not our expectations of what should be happening' and it was important to 'let them have time to be a child'. She thought she couldn't look after the children if she 'didn't love them. You've got to have the ability to really care about them. If you think it's important, how they do and how they develop, you're going to put in that time and that effort.' This influenced how she interpreted the two-year-olds' offer:

> *I think with the two-year-old funding as well, you're going to have some children who don't necessarily get, if not love, then the actual affection and the showing of love because some parents, they haven't been shown how to love and that is one of the fundamental things that children need to be able to develop.*

To summarise this figured world, Hilary employed expertise from her own experience as a parent as well as knowledge and experience gained through training and time working in nurseries; children took part in home-based activities and local days out, and relationships were those of friendship, love and support.

Community preschool

Context

All Saints preschool is a community group on the same site as (but separate from) a primary school in an inner city area. There were 19 funded two-years-olds on roll sharing the large open-plan hall and adjacent outside area with three- and four-year-olds. On the afternoon of my visit, six two-year-olds were engaged in table-top (playdough, action figures, jigsaw) and floor (minigym, ball play) activities inside and then also, from halfway through the session, climbing, bike and sand play outside. The two-year-olds moved freely between activities during the lively and cheerfully noisy session, interacting with staff who skilfully blended managing ('Be careful, that's Jack's picture') and extending ('they could be going to …') the children's involvement in activities.

Staff showed an enthusiastic and purposeful approach to professional development. The preschool manager held Early Years Professional Status (EYPS) and was studying for a Master's degree. This had given her more confidence, including the self-assurance to argue for her own reasoned opinion when external agencies or inspectors challenged aspects of provision. Other staff members were qualified to Level 3, except for a new entrant who had just embarked on Level 3. Recent whole-team professional development included language development, as well as training provided by the local authority for staff working with two-year-olds. In addition, the setting also offered work placements and apprenticeships for students from local schools; it was considered part of the setting's role to offer well-supported and appropriate routes into employment for people from the community. Staff also took part in strong local networks to stay up-to-date with policy developments and training opportunities.

Approach to provision for two-year-olds

To accommodate the increased number of younger children, staff were making changes to layout, routines and their general approach to interacting with two-year-olds. One staff member summed this up:

> *Clear communication; remembering to pitch at the right level; remembering to wait 10 seconds before responding; getting down to their level; working in smaller groups; in storytimes reminding other members of staff that they are only two and if they did manage two minutes sitting they should be allowed to get up and do something else. Patience; understanding to take the time; two-year-olds need time. Generally being laid-back and having a sense of calmness.*

Practitioners in this setting mentioned how an understanding of 'schemas' could help staff to think about the way two-year-olds enjoyed moving themselves (and other things) around the hall, and to make sure that this could be accommodated alongside the needs of other children (Brierley and Nutbrown, 2017). For example:

> *There's a time with children from the age of two especially, who transport equipment around the hall. So you could have a particular member of staff who thinks that things should stay on the table, but you've got to think of the needs of the child; the child might have a schema. That can be quite difficult because although the member of staff is aware of that — she knows to just let them carry it through because we can put it back — she is also looking at the three-year-olds who wanted to play with the puzzle game but can't because the two-year-old's come along and put it all in a little trolley and waltzed off. So it's being aware of it and trying to compromise and find a balance really.*

We've just got to be aware of their learning needs as well, whether it's 'transporting' or whatever. I think with doing observations on that child, you just find that transporting is a way of learning for them, then plan for that.

Staff were clear that the two-year-olds initiative offered the possibility of early intervention for children who were, for example, 'struggling with speech or behaviour' and that the progress check meant that this could be raised with parents. While the extra funding to enable children from disadvantaged homes to attend preschool was appreciated, there was nonetheless some ambivalence about the implications of the two-year-olds initiative for parents who might want to be at home with their children.

[If I was a parent] I'd like to decide whether I wanted that money so that I could put my child in a preschool for a day, or if I can have that extra money to not have to go to work for 15 hours a week, and spend that time with my child [...] I think women are slowly, slowly having these choices taken away.

Staff found that the two-year-olds funding offer and related policies could place them in a difficult position and disrupt their relationship with parents. For example, the local children's centre was distributing a 'goodie bag' to funded children, but the preschool had to sign a validating slip before parents were eligible. This cut across the setting's ethos of fairness and openness; because information about who was accessing two-year-olds funding was confidential, the setting was unable to explain to parents of unfunded children what was happening and why they weren't being offered a goodie bag.

A two-year-old attending this setting might therefore experience a figured world in which they found themselves in a large and lively space filled with children and adults, many of whom lived nearby, and where adults were learning about the knowledge and skills needed to work together and to help the preschool become ever better at supporting everyone's learning.

Rural daycare

Context

Meadowlands is a charitable organisation offering daycare in a rural setting on the edge of a village. The purpose-built centre is within a short walk of the local primary school, but also relatively close to a main cross-county route. This means that the setting has a wide catchment area, as parents can drop children off on their way to work elsewhere in the county. There are two playrooms, one for older children and another playroom with an adjacent sleeproom for children under three. Each playroom has an indoor messy area and easy access to its own outdoor area, with a large garden to the front of the building.

There is a stable staff team mostly trained to Level 3 or 4 and the manager has Early Years Professional Status (EYPS). The manager uses her network of contacts from different agencies to track down appropriate training, which had recently focused on language development, behaviour and child protection. Meadowlands is managed by a committee of volunteers including a large proportion of parents who use the setting. This helps to establish good relationships and ensures parents' ideas feed into planning.

Approach to provision for two-year-olds

The manager saw the two-year-olds funding as 'targeting families who need extra support', for example because of low income. She gave an example of one parent, a farm labourer, who had been taking her children along to work with her. The funding meant that the two-year-old was now able come to nursery instead. The manager also pointed out that children's speech and language difficulties tended to become evident as they approach two years and the two-year-olds funding meant settings could catch language difficulties early. This was an area where staff had been developing their knowledge and skills, although referrals for Speech and Language Therapy were not possible until children were aged three.

On the morning of my visit, there were ten two-year-olds, including three funded two-year-olds, and three babies in the younger children's playroom, who were moving between activities, between inside and outside, supported by staff in different ways (see Chapter 6). The children were absorbed by the mechanics of putting lids on things, pressing switches, collecting things, moving from place to place – and watching others. Practitioners facilitated these many separate 'mini-projects', enabling purposeful 'doing' without insisting on obvious end products. The manager flagged up the importance of staff, working in a room full of infants and toddlers, being able to adopt a consistent approach to behaviour and also to manage parents' concerns about behaviour (of their own and of other children). For her, this suggested the need for a different skill set for work in the younger children's room, echoing the comments by Karen's manager in Chapter 7.

This setting was meeting the needs of a diverse group of children and parents, so children met up with a variety of playmates from a wide geographical area and different social strata. Practitioners tended to work with a particular age group and their knowledge and training pathways reflected this.

Nursery unit in a school

Context

The final case study outlined in this chapter is a nursery unit within a primary school in one of the poorest wards in the city. The unit had had a previous life as an assessment centre for children with special educational needs. It was housed in a separate building with its own purpose-built outside area but shared some facilities with the school. There was a main playroom, a smaller 'quiet room' and a separate room for the two-year-olds – which was quickly abandoned as the two-year-olds

100 Jan Georgeson

'voted with their feet' and joined the main playroom after the beginning of the session (see Chapter 9 for another example of children's preferences shaping provision). There were eight two-year-olds attending this group, which had a relatively high proportion of children with special educational needs and children who were learning English as a second language.

The unit was staffed by an experienced and stable staff team with a wide range of qualifications, drawn from the local community. The manager explained how the mix of personnel contributed to good teamwork.

> So we have NNEB trained staff, we have NVQ 3 trained staff, we have a teacher, we have TAs [teaching assistants] who are not trained but have got experience. So that is our team. We work hopefully as a team and you build on people's strengths. So the people who are more theory-based you can bounce off with the people who are more practical-based so we learn from each other. I think that's the key.

Because of the unit's history as an assessment unit, there were strong connections with other agencies as well as good links with social services and the police.

Approach to provision for two-year-olds

The manager understood that the motivation for the two-year-olds funding was to 'narrow the gap':

> I think there's been research evidence that the children from more disadvantaged backgrounds have the most to gain from good high-quality provision, and child development in the early years is a more cost-effective way of improving individual economic and social outcomes.

But as well as addressing national priorities, the offer also fitted in with the setting's existing interest in possible ways to offer opportunities for two-year-olds from disadvantaged backgrounds to try out some of the activities their more advantaged peers might be doing already. The staff highlighted the importance of staff being skilful communicators and sensitive listeners:

> It's a number of ways of communication that's important – which is probably more important with the two-year-olds and we're thinking of the children we've got from other countries coming in here at the moment, really important.

They also reported that the sudden influx of two-year-olds had been a challenge to accommodate along with the needs of other vulnerable children, but that the mixed group was proving surprisingly successful:

> That whole span of ages and different skills, but they're very supportive of each other; it's wonderful.

> *It is. The only thing we have to make sure is our vulnerable three-year-olds are given the same attention as our two-year-olds, but every member is aware of that.*

However, despite this success, staff also felt that, in one respect, the two-year-olds initiative was a missed opportunity, because there was no funding for work with parents. In these extracts below from a focus group with the full staff group, staff explain the complexity of working with vulnerable two-year-olds and their families, again echoing comments made by the manager of Meadowlands and by the manager quoted at the end of Chapter 7:

> BELLE: *I would say for me I think it is very good for the children to be in with us and I hope we are impacting on their lives in a positive way, but I still think we need to be doing more with the parents and more groups with the parents, helping parents with having positive routines.*
>
> ZOE: *Helping parents have the time for their children, to improve their skills in order to parent their children well.*
>
> ETHEL: *Can I just say that I think we are providing and it is working out, but from a personal view I think two-year-olds are nicer with their mums and if you could give parents the tools to take them to the park — mums or dads to spend that time and enjoy them — to me that is where I think two-year-olds personally should be.*
>
> BELLE: *Get them to enjoy them, get them to take them through all their routines for their day, to help them with their bedtime routine, what's appropriate, having lovely stories at bedtime, having a lovely bath time. I would just like to be able to give that to all the parents out there so that they can enjoy those times really.*
>
> RONNIE: *But parents should not be criticised. You've got to get that real big bit of trust before they are opening up.*
>
> BELLE: *To be honest, we don't want to be putting them down and criticising and saying 'you should be …'. We'll have a laugh and a joke but they know that they can call on us and they know that we would help them. And they do rely on us a lot; it's a very family-orientated school.*

In this figured world, children found themselves in a setting that was very different from their homes, but with children and staff who lived near them, some of whom they know through family connections and some they did not. Staff in this setting had a strong sense of their mission to support children's development and so catch up with other children by the time they started school, and to involve parents in this mission.

These four contexts, therefore, prioritised different aspects of the two-year-olds' offer; staff saw it as an opportunity to address needs that they had often already identified in their communities. Their construction of two-year-olds in need of a funded place picked up elements of vulnerability outlined in Chapter 3, and also displayed an awareness of the tensions inherent in recognising these needs while not stigmatising child or family, to try to create the 'coherent spaces' of discourse advocated in Chapter 5. In the following chapters we move beyond the *Two-year-olds in*

102 Jan Georgeson

England project to look at other spaces for two-year-olds, and the different figured worlds which they might encounter.

Questions

Are the practitioners in the settings described here acquiring the same knowledges about working with two-year olds? What might happen if they were to swap roles for a day?

Further reading

Georgeson, J. M. (2010). Diverse needs, different provision; how differences in preschool settings support children to learn how to be learners. In Daniels, H. and Hedegaard, M. (eds.), *Vygotsky and Special Needs Education*. London: Continuum, 191–206.

This chapter uses four case studies to show how different forms of provision can support children in different ways, arguing that local practitioners in local settings are well placed to provide preschool experiences that are best matched to local children's needs.

References

Brierley, J. and Nutbrown, C. (2017). *Understanding Schematic Learning at Two*. London: Bloomsbury.

Georgeson, J., Campbell-Barr, V., Boag-Munroe, G., Mathers, S., Caruso, F. and Parker-Rees, R. (2014). *Two-year-olds in England: An Exploratory Study*. London: TACTYC.

Holland, D., Lachiocotte, W., Skinner, D. and Cain, C. (1998). *Identity and Agency in Cultural Worlds*. Cambridge, MA: Harvard University Press.

Penn, H. (2009). International perspectives on quality in mixed economies of childcare. *National Institute Economic Review*, 207(1), 83–89.

9
ENVIRONMENTS FOR LISTENING

Karen Wickett

Introduction

In this chapter I share the experiences of practitioners from three Sure Start Children's Centre (SSCC) settings, as they changed the physical environment and practices of the education and care provision for the youngest children. In two settings an internal wall was knocked down and in the third setting practices were beginning to be developed in the garden. The motivation to change the environments and practices was the belief that the voices of the children in the baby/two-and-a-half-year-old room and of those caring for them were not being heard. To gain insights into the practitioners' experiences of working with the youngest children and the changes, Jan Georgeson and I interviewed the practitioners. Each setting had a unique journey, as practitioners changed the environment and practices. The changes led to shifts in the pedagogic discourse, the rules of behaviour shaping the experiences of children and adults (Bernstein, 2000).

Chapters 1 and 4 have already outlined the policy context for the provision of the places for two-year-olds, and how funded early years provision for two-year-olds is a relatively new feature of early years policy in England. The neglect of focus on two-year-olds has two consequences that are pertinent to this chapter; firstly, that there has been a historical lack of provision for younger children, due to the focus on provision for three- and four-year-olds. Secondly, the historical split model of childcare for the youngest children and early education for three- and four-year-olds has had a lasting legacy. Importantly, the division between those who work with children over three years and those who work with the under-threes was exacerbated by the terms and conditions of those working with the under-threes, with minimal opportunities for career development, fewer experiences, and a concern that this could lead to feelings of being undervalued, unsupported and

The political educational readiness discourse

The historical divide between those working with the very youngest children and three- and four-year-olds was noted over 20 years ago by Goldschmied and Jackson, but so too were the influences of the schooling system in shaping provision for the youngest children.

> [P]roviding for the cognitive development of even the youngest children is a central aspect of the nursery worker's task. There are already signs that this is happening. Probably the majority of centres where under-twos are cared for already have a separate room for them.
>
> (Goldschmied and Jackson, 1994: 20)

Before children were divided by age, they were cared for in mixed-aged groups (Goldschmied and Jackson, 1994). Caring for and educating children by age are practices associated with school. The revised Early Years Foundation Stage (EYFS; DfE, 2014) continues to reinforce these practices: 'Except in childminding settings, there should be a separate baby room for children under the age of two' (DfE, 2014:28). It is common practice in Early Childhood Education and Care (ECEC) settings that children are accommodated in different rooms depending on their age.

Separating children into groups by age can position the very youngest children, their practitioners and the knowledge about young children's learning at the bottom of the 'epistemological hierarchy' (Urban, 2008). The hierarchical nature of schooling views children moving from the bottom (ECEC) to the top (secondary school and beyond) (Moss, 2013). Thus, the purpose of the ECEC sector is to prepare children for school learning. Moss terms this as the readiness relationship (Moss, 2013). In this relationship the flow of communication is generally in one direction from the top to the bottom (Moss, 2013: 4), and the information shared by those from above is what is expected of children for the next phase of their education trajectory. The low status of the ECEC practitioners can explain why they believe they are unnoticed and unheard.

It is not only practitioners that can be silenced in the current readiness discourse. Children can also be expected to be silent. Former Minister of Education and Childcare, Liz Truss, explained that to be ready for school children should 'learn to listen to a teacher, learn to respect an instruction' (Gov.uk, 2013). Although some may expect children to listen, others view it is important and necessary to listen to children.

ECEC pioneers encouraged those working with the children to listen and notice what children are doing when planning environments and experiences for them (Andrews and Wickett, 2015). Lorenzo Malaguzzi, the founder of the pre-schools of Reggio Emilia, advocated listening to children's '100 languages'.

Practitioners are encouraged to engage in the active process of listening by 'seeing, talking and acting in a different way' (Rinaldi, 1994, cited in Scott, 2001: 23), viewing learning as a social process in which children and adults listen to each other's theories, and engage in the process of meaning-making. Listening to children is not only at the practitioner level in localised approaches like Reggio Emilia; it is also reflected in global discourse through *The United Nations Rights of the Child*, where Article 12 states that children have 'the right to be heard' and consulted with when developing provision (UN, 1989). The convention challenged the view that children should be 'seen and not heard', instead viewing them active as participants who were competent and capable of making decisions about their lives.

Listening

The discussion above has highlighted that in English societies speaking dominates listening (Back, 2007), and it is generally those with the appropriate authority and knowledge who are listened to (Belenky et al., 1986). Listening becomes a passive activity, when instead listening should be an active process, but this can be challenging. Listening can be difficult as hearing other people's perspectives can challenge our own. Instead of judging and dismissing these perspectives, active listening encourages those listening to value difference, consider other possibilities and engage in the process of meaning-making (Dahlberg et al., 1999). Throughout the listening process, children and adults not only listen with their ears but also have 'wide eyes and open minds' (Nutbrown, 1996: 44).

Listening is of great importance to me; not only am I the author of this paper and a member of the research team, but I was also the Children's Centre teacher in the Castleton setting, one of the three settings described here. Prior to starting my role in the Children's Centre a defining moment for me was during my final teaching practice in an ECEC setting when I took a moment to listen to a two-year-old.

I had previously observed a two-year-old boy standing on the dais looking over a picket fence from the quiet area, where the two-year-olds were generally located, into the main space of the setting. I had noticed him watching the other children as they played and went about their lives. He had done this for over a period of two weeks. Today he climbed down from the dais, walked to the gate, opened it and tottered into the main space. The two-year-old strutted around the room confidently with his chest puffed out. After a while he returned to the sanctuary of the quiet area. The toddler had planned his own transition from the quiet area to the main part of the setting. His world had widened. He was now able to access the rest of the setting provision inside and outside as he required.

> In the above scenario, the physical environment and systems in the setting enabled the two-year-old to move from one area to another when he chose. He was also able to control and decide when he was ready, physically, emotionally and socially, to participate in this space. He was developing a positive sense of self and identity and he had an understanding of his abilities and limitations. There were no rules stipulating the age or developmental stage that the child should be at when he moved from the two-year-olds room to the pre-school room. Instead, the only rule was the practitioners should listen to the children in order to become aware of their decisions and intentions, and support them during their self-directed challenges.

Changes within the settings

Castleton setting

My learning from the above scenario stayed with me. When I started my position in the Children's Centre I often thought of the two-year-old planning his transition between the ECEC setting spaces. When observing the younger children in the Castleton toddler room, I often noticed them looking over the metal gate into the pre-school room, and sometimes they would cry and shake the gate. In such circumstances a baby-room practitioner who noticed the child crying would carry them back into the room and distract them until they were settled. I wondered, 'is this really what the child wanted?', and realised how the spaces we provide for children can silence their voices.

In time, when the team had an opportunity to consider and develop their practices, we wrote down the setting's principles. It was striking that members of the team had felt unheard in the past and were determined to ensure all members of the ECEC setting were listened to. One of the principles stated as a team was that we would:

> *listen to each other and ensure that everyone is able to make themselves understood. We are positive in our responses, providing support and encouragement for the individual.*
> (Castleton setting Principles, 2006)

After the principles had been written, I shared my observations and thoughts about the younger children crying at the metal gate with the team. Later during a conversation with the manager she suggested knocking down the wall between the rooms so the younger children could use the whole space when they felt ready. Soon afterwards the wall was knocked down and the children were able to see into and move between the rooms via a gate in a wooden fence (see Figure 9.1). This was four years before the research was conducted.

Environments for listening **107**

FIGURE 9.1 The children were able to see into and move between the rooms via a gate in a wooden fence

Parkside setting

Originally the Parkside setting was established as a local pre-school. The children attended the setting from two-and-a-half years until they went to school. In 2006 the setting became part of the Children's Centre and was then registered for babies from four months old. Children under two-and-a-half years were based in one room and the older children in the pre-school room. Yet, all children shared the garden and ate together at mealtimes. I had discussed integrating younger and older children with the manager when the building was being constructed, but at that time she could not perceive how this might work. After studying, reflecting and observing the practice in the setting her thinking changed, particularly when she noticed a division between the practitioners:

> *There was a babies/two-year-olds team and a pre-school team … those caring for the younger children always felt a bit isolated and [that] their work wasn't as important as the rest of the nursery. So that was my main reason for getting the wall down. So the staff team would feel more part of one nursery because we are all one team and one nursery.*
>
> (Ruby, Parkside practitioner)

108 Karen Wickett

Eighteen months prior to the research, she had shared her idea with the team and six months later the wall came down and a picket fence was put up.

Treetops setting

In this setting, the babies/two-year-olds are separated from the pre-school children. A picket fence and gate divide the spaces. The two-year-olds did not access the pre-school room until the practitioner believed the children were ready for the transition. At the time of the research, the outside area was being developed so the younger children could mix with the pre-school children. The new manager had introduced these practices.

Methodology

I believe people are social actors who, with the groups they belong to, construct knowledge and views of the world in their historical and cultural context (Benzies and Allen, 2001; Burr, 2003). In keeping with views that the construction of knowledge and culture is a social process (Burr, 2003: 20), this epistemological position aligns with socio-cultural theories of knowledge construction (Rogoff, 2003). Therefore, Jan and I designed interviews which drew upon aspects of narrative enquiry. Narrative enquiry illuminates participants' experiences that have shaped their beliefs and views of the world (Clandinin and Connelly, 1996; Court et al., 2009). Practitioners were asked to 'share their stories of being with and working with babies and very young children'.

Classification and framing

To guide the analysis of the data we used Bernstein's concepts of 'classification and framing' (2000: 99). These provided a lens to make sense of the structures and systems that affected the children's and adults' experiences, communication and relationships during the changes to the environment. The concept of classification considers the relationships between groups (Bernstein, 2000). The insulation of the boundary between groups can be strong or weak, which will influence the classification between groups (Bernstein, 2000). If classification is strong then there will be distinct groups. The power relationships between the groups 'create, legitimise and reproduce symbolic boundaries between different groups' (Singh, 1997: 5). The concept of framing can also be strong or weak but refers to the control of communication (Bernstein, 1996: 26) between those in the group. Framing studies the nature of control in a group by exploring the communicative practices that are carried out between transmitters and acquirers (Bernstein, 2000). Framing will determine the types of communication and behaviour of those in the group as 'it is concerned with how meanings are put together, the forms by which they are to be made public, and the nature of the social relationships' (Bernstein, 2000: 27). If there is strong framing then the experiences for the children and adults will be like formal schooling, when

Environments for listening **109**

knowledge and skills are transmitted from the teacher to the pupil. In such contexts, the pedagogy is visible (Bernstein, 2000). If on the other hand the framing is weak, the relationship between the learner and teacher is less marked, the learner's voice is listened to and they have an element of control and influence over the content of the curriculum. These practices are termed 'invisible pedagogy' (Bernstein, 2000).

Bernstein (2000: 45) identified two general pedagogic models: the performance model (strong classification and framing) and the competence model (weak classification and framing). The practices of visible pedagogy are attributed to the performance model, which often underpins primary and secondary education. Invisible pedagogy relates to the competence model, which generally underpins the practices of ECEC. Although Bernstein identified these two models, he recognised that there were many forms and variations of practice. He used the term 'pedagogic pallet' (Bernstein, 2000) to describe the range of pedagogic practices. The shade of pedagogy is dependent on the strength and weakness of the classification and framing in the school. I therefore draw on Bernstein to consider how, during the changes in the ECEC settings, the shades on the pedagogic pallet changed.

Classification

Two-year-olds and pre-school children

Before the physical environments of the ECEC settings were changed, there was strong classification between those in the baby/two-year-old room and those in the pre-school room. Flo and Marie explained:

> *it was quite separate for two years I worked alongside … a girl and we worked together just with the babies and two-year-olds.*
>
> (Flo, Castleton practitioner)

> *we had our own space, that was always quite nice and there was the chance to really cut off, because it can get very noisy.*
>
> (Marie, Parkside practitioner)

The terms 'separate' and 'cut off' suggest Flo and Marie saw themselves and the youngest children as a distinct group from the others in the setting. Marie viewed being able to cut themselves off from the rest of the setting as positive, particularly when it was noisy. It is not clear if the noise came from the pre-school or two-year-old room. The physical pedagogic space and shutting the door reinforced the classification between the youngest children and the pre-school children.

Since the changes to the environment, the classification has weakened. The youngest children are able to move between spaces.

> *to have an open environment like that it gave them [children] the opportunity to wander in and out as they pleased.*
>
> (Marie, Parkside practitioner)

110 Karen Wickett

This time Marie describes the environment as 'open', enabling the children to have control and decide when they move between the spaces. They did not just decide when to move into the main area (previously the pre-school room) but they also decided how long to spend in this space and when to move back to the quiet area (previously the two-year-old room). It was not only the younger children using the whole environment but also the pre-school children. The older children also used the quiet area. Poppy explains:

> the bigger children like to come in and lie down if they are feeling a bit tired as well … and if they want to take a book in there then they can. But they do understand that they need to be quiet, if they are not going to sleep then they need to be quiet and they are really good at doing that.
>
> (Poppy, Parkside practitioner)

Poppy's comments demonstrate that the changes in the physical environment provide opportunities for children, regardless of their age, to move between the spaces dependent on how they felt and what they wanted to do. The changes have weakened the classification between the groups of children. Instead, the spaces in the room have become strongly classified. The children were aware that different spaces required certain behaviours.

Practitioners also changed the labels that they used when referring to those in their care. Vanessa explained:

> it is another way of looking at babies … seeing it less as babies, two-year-olds and pre-schoolers but actually as children.
>
> (Vanessa, Castleton practitioner)

Instead of labelling individual groups, which reinforced the classification between the groups of children, all of them were labelled 'children' regardless of their age.

Baby/two-year-old practitioners and pre-school practitioners

In the Parkside setting the classification between children weakened, but there was less of a change in the classification between the groups of practitioners. Poppy explained:

> I was in the big room for a little bit but now I've been put back in, obviously with my experience with them … I've been more in the little ones' room.
>
> (Poppy, Parkside practitioner)

Although the wall was down and the physical space was seen as one room, practitioners were still responsible for either the quiet area or activity area. Such systems can reinforce practitioners' roles and the classification between groups of practitioners.

Environments for listening **111**

In Parkside, another system that remained after the changes was the key-person role. Younger children were allocated a key-person when they started at the setting and then when they reached two-and-a-half years they had a new key-person. Practitioners in the quiet area were a key-person for the younger children and the other practitioners were a key-person for the older children. This could be problematic at times for the practitioner based in the quiet area:

> *sometimes it's OK, when the bigger ones can come in and sometimes it's not. I think they came in as babies some of them and it's where they have always been and I think it's their comfort zone … If they are feeling a little bit unsure they come back to that area.*

> (April, Parkside practitioner)

April posed a possible reason why the older children returned to this area. Although the older children had a key-person who was based in the activity area, the children still returned to her when they needed emotional comfort. An explanation for this is she had been their original key-person and the strength of the relationship remained.

In the Castleton setting, the practices of the key-person had changed:

> *They would change key-person as well. [Since the wall came down]… the key-person [is the same] from three months up to school age.*

> (Vanessa, Castleton practitioner)

Prior to the wall coming down, the children would change rooms and key-person, but since the wall came down children had the same key-person from the day they started at the setting until the day they left. As each practitioner had older and younger children, practitioners were no longer expected to be based in one area. Instead, practitioners used the whole environment depending on the state of their key-children. Lily explained:

> *you just accompany them … we have had a few children who have been really clinging towards an adult and we've just had to compensate for that, just allow time for that adult to spend time with [their] key-child.*

> (Lily, Castleton practitioner)

Whilst the practitioners were responsible for emotionally supporting their key-children, the rest of the practitioners supported their colleague by enabling them to have time with the unsettled child in the space that suited the child. This had implications for the whole team as they all moved around the environment, as they had to be aware of each other and what was happening in the environment.

112 Karen Wickett

As practitioners were able to move between spaces to support the children, it also brought variation in their role:

> *I kind of like sometimes to spend time with the youngest children, kind of the calm moment, and then I like spending time with the older ones with the big running around.*
>
> (Sophie, Castleton practitioner)

The flexible environment and diversity in practitioners' role also led David to believe:

> *We don't get segregated, we don't get treated differently and you all mingle like a large family.*
>
> (David, Castleton practitioner)

The classification between baby/two-year-old practitioners and pre-school practitioners had weakened, which enabled practitioners to 'mingle' with each other.

In both Parkside and Castleton ECEC settings the classification between those in the baby/two-year-old room and pre-school room had weakened. In Parkside, however, the boundary strength had weakened mostly between the groups of children, as they could move between spaces. The boundary strength between the baby/two-year-old room and pre-school room adults did not weaken as much as the practices, such as areas of responsibility and key-person system, which limited the opportunities for practitioners to move between spaces. Consequently, the classification between the groups of adults was slightly stronger than in Castleton where the systems had been developed in light of the changes to the physical environment. In the Castleton setting, the weak classification between practitioners provided opportunities for them to move around the setting. This flexibility and the view of the environment as one enabled practitioners to move when they were required to meet the ratio requirements.

It was not only the setting's systems but also the practitioners' emotional needs that reinforced the strength of classification between practitioners:

> *I sort of started going out but I was still based in that room; I'd go back to my comfort zone.*
>
> (Flo, Castleton practitioner)

Flo explained that she had returned to the area where she felt most comfortable. A part of the adjustment process was for ECEC practitioners to reconstruct their identity and understanding of their role. Lily remembers this time:

> *[the changes were] very different for us, so we had to overcome that and it was more our thing than, you know – the younger [children] were just exploring everything! We had to get more comfortable with ourselves as being able to watch them.*
>
> (Lily, Castleton practitioner)

Not only were practitioners constructing new identities, but also their roles changed as did their views of the children. The new environment provided new opportunities for the younger children to explore and the new role for the practitioner was to observe and listen to the children exploring instead of limiting these opportunities. Lily realised she had to acclimatise to the changes. Part of this adjustment period for Flo was to move back and forth between the spaces. Flo also explained:

> *We had quite a lot of discussions and I suppose it was their [manager and teacher] support as well and then actually seeing how the older children were interacting with the younger children − actually going out with the younger children and seeing.*
>
> (Flo, Castleton practitioner)

In this context, the leaders had provided opportunities to explore these challenges through the processes of dialogue, reflection and watching the children. The process enabled practitioners to construct new understandings of children, their role in supporting them and views about environments for children's learning.

In Treetops, the classification remained strong between groups. The practitioners were at the beginning of their journey to integrate the children and practitioners. Alannah (Treetops practitioner) explains: '*Well, we could use the big room a bit more.*' She is considering other ways of providing environments for children.

Framing

Communication

In the Castleton setting before the wall was knocked down, if a child stood at the gate crying, the practitioner would move them away and distract them. Since the changes, practitioners recognised 'the 100 languages of children' (Malaguzzi, 1993) and considered other possible meanings behind the child's behaviours.

> *When they start crawling they usually go to the gate and sort of shake the gate, so you kind of know that they want to go out. So we just open it and let them go and obviously we watch them.*
>
> (Sophie, Castleton practitioner)

Sophie explained how she actively watched and listened to the child's actions and now heard that the child wanted to move between spaces.

Just like the physical environment, the systems and structures can limit the practitioners being able to actively listen to the children. In the Treetops setting, Alannah explained:

> *older ones in the baby room tend to dominate play and attention and a lot of the boisterous boys, well and girls. There are some that are so ready for that next step but they*

114 Karen Wickett

> *are not quite old enough to be in our room and they get a bit bored so they bring it out in negative behaviour to get attention.*
>
> (Alannah, Treetops practitioner)

Alannah acknowledged that the children were communicating boredom and a desire to move rooms, but she was unable to respond, as the setting rules had stipulated that these children were not old enough to move to the pre-school room.

Pacing, sequencing and criteria

The environment and rules can lead to practitioners controlling the pace, sequence and criteria of activities. In the Treetops setting, practitioners lead the pace, sequence and the criteria during the transition.

> *When they hit two-and-a-half it was sort of you are up there … we could take them through [to the pre-school-room] and take them away out the little room and maybe sit and do painting in there. So that they are used to being in that room in a small group.*
>
> (Alannah, Treetops practitioner)

The setting's systems reinforced the strength of the framing between practitioners and children. It is the practitioner who determines the pace and sequencing of the transition. Alannah does explain that there are opportunities to consider different processes in response to the children.

In contrast, when the wall came down in Parkside, practitioners listened to the children and supported them to plan the transition between rooms.

> *when they are old enough and confident enough to go up to the gate and go that little bit further into the big wide world.*
>
> (Ruby, Parkside practitioner)

Ruby is aware that it is not only the children's age that can determine when they are ready for the move but also their confidence.

There is evidence in both Parkside and Castleton settings that practitioners view children as capable of planning their transition and that the transition is a process. In these settings, children can decide when they move between spaces and how long they stay in each space. The role of the practitioner is to accompany the children in the Castleton setting.

The control over the social base

The changes in environment had led to Castleton practitioners becoming aware that children were not only capable learners and effective communicators, but also that children and practitioners were learning together. David had noticed that older children were effective at supporting the younger children to learn new skills:

> *I see them pick up so much more from more children of their age range. Because they have recently gone through that stage so they obviously understand their level of thinking better than obviously ourselves. Because they have recently experienced learning to climb up the climbing frame; they have just learnt to kick a ball.*
>
> (David, Castleton practitioner)

Whilst the younger children were learning from the older children, the older children were learning how to support younger children through observation of adults.

> *I've witnessed a four-year-old and a two-year-old sitting together engaged. The four-year-old will be mimicking what the two-year-old said but that is the kind of thing that an adult would do. That was just amazing to watch because the four-year-old had picked up on what the two-year-old was doing and obviously picked up on how we respond to younger children when we do that and it was just amazing.*
>
> (Lily, Castleton practitioner)

In turn, the practitioners were also learning from the children as well. Both of the practitioners above experienced moments of awe as they learnt about children supporting each other to learn and the influences that adults have on children.

Unique settings, unique pedagogic practices

Each setting's pedagogic practices had a unique shade on the pedagogic pallet (Bernstein, 2000), with varying strengths of classification and framing. There was strong classification and framing in the Treetops setting; the classification between groups was strong, as there were two distinct rooms and two groups of children and practitioners. Framing was also strong as the environment and the setting's systems influenced how practitioners heard what the children were communicating. Instead of hearing the children's behaviour expressing that they wanted to move between rooms, their behaviour was labelled as boisterous. The systems also reinforced the baby/two-year-old practitioners' control over when the children could access the provision in the pre-school room.

In Parkside, the classification and framing between the baby/two-year-old and pre-school room participants had weakened due to changes in the environment. The older and younger children were able to decide when to use and move between the different spaces. Practitioners viewed children, regardless of their age, as competent in making such decisions and would listen to them as they moved around the setting. Whilst the classification between the younger and older children had weakened, the classification between the groups of practitioners remained relatively strong. The setting's systems, such as changing key-person when the child was

116 Karen Wickett

a certain age and areas of responsibility for practitioners, limited the opportunities for practitioners to move between each space and also to be viewed as one group.

The Castleton setting had weak classification and framing between the practitioners and children. Changes in the physical environment also led to the development of the structures and systems, children having one key-person throughout this phase of education, and the development of practitioners' areas of responsibility. Practitioners were not responsible for one room in the setting but for their key-children. These changes have resulted in baby/two-year-old practitioners and pre-school practitioners all being called practitioners and younger or older children called children. There was flexibility for children and practitioners to move around the setting and for all to listen to each other.

Power

During the change process, power between children/children, practitioners/practitioners and practitioners/children became more evenly distributed. It could, however, be argued that the leaders of the settings silenced some practitioners' voices when initiating the change. As advocates for young children, leaders and practitioners should challenge existing practices (Bae, 2010) and develop new ways of providing environments for two-year-old children and those who care for them. If practices are not challenged, practitioners can be trapped in traditional understandings of children and practice (Bae, 2010). This could continue to marginalise some children's and practitioners' voices.

New ways of looking at the world

In this study, during the messy process of change practitioners encountered challenges. Bernstein (2000: 6) recognised that 'if the insulation is broken, then the category is in danger of losing its identity'. This was the case in Castleton as Lily recounted: '*we had to get more comfortable with ourselves*'. Lily and her colleagues engaged in the process of reconstructing their identities as they were no longer either a baby/two-year-old or pre-school practitioner but ECEC practitioners. A role for leaders is to support this process of meaning-making by creating environments for 'dialogue, reflection, celebration of differences, containment and challenge' (Whalley et al., 2008: 10). Enabling practitioners to engage in this process is likely to transform their views of themselves, their values and practice (Argyris and Schon, 1996). Changing their views of themselves consequently led to practitioners changing how they viewed the children as communicators and their role in the process of listening and hearing. In contexts where there was weak classification and framing, practitioners were engaging in the process of actively listening to children. When actively listening to the children, practitioners considered other possible meanings and were more likely to respond as the children wanted.

Not only were there changes in practitioners' views of children as communicators but also as learners. The changes in the environment and systems highlighted

Environments for listening **117**

for the practitioners that children were competent and capable at exploring and making sense of the world. Instead of controlling the learning processes, the practitioners became aware that they were learning alongside the children and that children were effective teachers for their peers. Practitioners viewed their role as facilitators in children's exploration and partners in the process of meaning-making (Dahlberg et al., 1999).

Conclusion

This chapter began by considering how ECEC and ECEC practitioners are at the bottom of the epistemological hierarchy, where they might believe they are undervalued and unheard. This study found that the physical environment can reinforce their position at the bottom of the epistemological hierarchy and limit opportunities for practitioners and children to be heard. The layout of the physical environment can either reinforce the ages and stages concept of development or offer other possibilities such as an environment that listens to the children's '100 languages' (Malaguzzi, 1993). In these environments, children and practitioners are active participants in the 'democratic process of collective decision-making' (Moss, 2007: 9) in how the space is used and the design of the curriculum (Emilson and Folkesson, 2006).

A role for leaders is to challenge but still support practitioners by encouraging them to engage in the process of dialogue and reflection to consider different ways of working. Part of this process is for practitioners to challenge current beliefs and understandings of children, learning and their role, and make links with theory (Goouch and Powell, 2011). Although this can be an uncomfortable process, by engaging in the process of meaning-making (Ball, 2011; Goouch and Powell, 2011) practitioners can create environments, systems and structures that reflect their beliefs about children, learning and themselves.

It is likely that such practices will create stronger boundaries between ECEC settings and formal schooling. The strengthening of the classification can cause tensions between these groups. Moss (2007) encourages ECEC practitioners to challenge the discourses that characterise the readiness relationship (see Chapter 5), particularly at a time when the youngest children are the focus of government policy. It is important that ECEC practitioners challenge the dominance of the 'education' discourse to ensure the youngest children and those caring for them are listened to when creating enabling learning environments (DfE, 2014). These environments are then more likely to provide opportunities for children to foster their skills, knowledge and dispositions for learning for life and school.

Questions

Imagine you are a child who attends your/an early years setting. What opportunities are there for you to be actively listened to and heard by the adults/children in the setting?

118 · Karen Wickett

Identify a space in the setting and consider how the children communicate. How does the environment shape how and what they communicate?

On the one hand, education policies expect us to listen to children and on the other hand, there are policies that can silence children. How do you and your colleagues negotiate these contradictory expectations?

Further reading

Rinaldi, C. (2012).The pedagogy of listening: The listening perspective from Reggio Emilia in Edwards, C., Gandini, L. and Forman, G. (eds.), *The Hundred Languages of Children.The Reggio Emilia Experience of Transformation* (3rd ed.) Oxford: Praeger.

In this chapter Carlina Rinaldi focuses on the differences between the kind of research that takes place in scientific laboratories and universities, and the kind of research or experimentation that teachers and ordinary citizens can and should do 'a way of thinking for ourselves and thinking jointly with others, a way of relating with other people, with the world around us, and with life' (p. 245).

References

Andrews, M. and Wickett, K. (2015). Observing children:The importance of personal insight and reflective action, in Parker-Rees, R. and Leeson, C. (eds.), *Early Childhood Studies:An Introduction to the Study of Children's Lives and Children's Worlds* (4th ed.). London: Sage, 73–84.

Argyris, C. and Schon, D. (1996). *Organizational Learning 2: Theory, Method and Practice.* New York: Addison-Wesley Publishing Company.

Back, L. (2007). *The Art of Listening.* Oxford: Berg Publishers.

Bae, B. (2010). Realising children's right to participate in early childhood settings: Some critical issues in a Norwegian context, *Early Years*, 30(3) 205–218.

Ball, S. J. (2011).Teachers as actors/teachers as subjects: Dealing with policy contradictions and contradictory policies!! University of Exeter Seminar Series, 22 February 2011.

Belenky, M. F., Clinchy, B. M., Goldberg, N. R. and Tarule, J. M. (1986). *Women's Ways of Knowing: The Development of Self, Voice, and Mind.* New York: Basic Books.

Benzies, K. M. and Allen, M. N. (2001). Symbolic interactionism as a theoretical perspective for multiple method research, *Journal of Advanced Nursing*, 33(4), 541–547.

Bernstein, B. (1996). *Pedagogy Symbolic Control and Identity: Theory, Research, Critique.* London: Taylor and Francis.

Bernstein, B. (2000). *Pedagogy Symbolic Control and Identity:Theory, Research, Critique* (rev. ed.). Oxford: Rowman and Littlefield.

Burr,V. (2003). *Social Constructionism* (2nd ed.). Hove: Routledge.

Clandinin, J. D. and Connelly, F. M. (1996). Teachers' professional knowledge landscapes: Teacher stories – stories of teachers – school stories – stories of school, *Educational Researcher*, 25(3), 24–30.

Court, D., Merav, L. and Ornan, E. (2009). Preschool teachers' narratives: A window on personal-professional history, values and beliefs, *International Journal of Early Years Education*, 17(3), 207–217.

Dahlberg, G., Moss, P. and Pence, A. (1999). *Beyond Quality in Early Childhood Education and Care: Postmodern Perspectives.* London: Routledge/Falmer.

Department for Education (DfE) (2014). *Statutory Framework for the Early Years Foundation Stage: Setting the Standards for Learning, Development and Care for Children from Birth to Five.* London: DfE.

Emilson, A. and Folkesson, A-M. (2006). Children's participation and teacher control, *Early Child Development and Care*, 176(3–4), 219–238.

Goldschmied, E. and Jackson, S. (1994) *People under Three: Young Children in Day Care.* London: Routledge.

Goouch, K. and Powell, S. (2011) *The Baby Room Project.* TACTYC Reflections paper. Available at http://tactyc.org.uk/pdfs/Reflection-Goouch.pdf (Accessed on: 27/07/2017).

Gov.uk (2013). Elizabeth Truss speaks about 2-year-olds policy and practice. DfE. Available at: www.gov.uk/government/speeches/elizabeth-truss-speaks-about-2-year-olds-policy-and-practice (Accessed on: 17/09/2017).

Malaguzzi, L. (1993). The hundred languages of children, in Edwards, C., Gardini, L. and Foreman, G. (eds.), *The Hundred Languages of Children.* Norwood: Ablex, 41–90.

Moss, P. (2007). Bringing politics into the nursery: Early childhood education as a democratic practice, *European Early Childhood Education Research Journal*, 15(1), 5–20.

Moss, P. (ed.) (2013). *Early Childhood and Compulsory Education: Reconceptualising the Relationship.* Abingdon: Routledge.

Nutbrown, P. C. (1996). *Respectful Educators – Capable Learners: Children's Rights and Early Education.* London: Sage.

Rogoff, B. (2003). *The Cultural Nature of Human Development.* Oxford: Oxford University Press.

Scott, W. (2001). Listening and learning, in Abbott, L. and Nutbrown, C. (eds.), *Experiencing Reggio Emilia: Implications for Pre-School Provision.* London: Routledge, 21–29.

Singh, P. (1997). Review essay: Basil Bernstein (1996) Pedagogy, symbolic control and identity, *British Journal of Sociology of Education*, 18(1), 119–124.

United Nations (UN) (1989). *UN Convention on the Rights of the Child.* Available at: www.unicef.org/crc/files/Rights_overview.pdf (Accessed on: 08/08/2017).

Urban, M. (2008). Dealing with uncertainty: Challenges and possibilities for the early childhood profession, *European Early Childhood Education Research Journal*, 16(2), 135–152.

Whalley, M., Chandler, R., John, K., Reid, L., Thorpe, S. and Everitt, J. (2008). Developing and sustaining leadership learning communities: Implications of NPQICL rollout of public policy local praxis, *European Early Childhood Education Research Journal*, 16(1), 5–38.

10

INSPIRING WORK WITH BIRTH-TO-TWOS

A creative and cultural perspective

Clare Halstead

Introduction

Visitors to the Towner Gallery in Eastbourne on a Tuesday morning might be surprised to see small children and their parents taking off their shoes and disappearing into a large fabric tent in a room on the first floor. At the Jerwood Gallery in Hastings, there is a weekly queue of buggies outside waiting to get in for an early session before the gallery opens its doors to the public. And the Hastings Museum and Art Gallery has been welcoming under-fives with specially designed activities for more than 12 years.

In 2014 and 2015, all three cultural venues collaborated with artists and with staff from local Children's Centres on ways to work with families with children from birth to two years and to develop partnerships through an innovative creative project called Open Sesame, developed and managed by the arts education organisation Culture Shift (Culture Shift, no date). Through a series of three projects in Sussex and Surrey, Open Sesame has been developing an approach to support creative collaboration between the early years and arts sectors, encourage the development of creative skills in early years practitioners and settings, and support artists to gain experience for work in early years settings. These projects were funded by Arts Council England (including Creative Partnerships), county council early years and arts services and individual early years settings, supported in-kind by a range of cultural and early years partners and managed through these partnerships and by Culture Shift Community Interest Company.

Most arts organisations receiving public funding will be aiming to be as inclusive as they can and work with the widest possible audiences. Working with under-fives is an important part of this approach, and there are some shining examples of groundbreaking work taking place – for example, the Whitworth Museum in Manchester (University of Manchester, no date). A report for King's College

A creative and cultural perspective **121**

London that looked at the development of arts policy towards children and young people (Doeser, 2015) recommended that 'policy-makers place greater emphasis on encouraging arts activity amongst pre-school-aged children' (p. 24) and links this directly to family participation and the positive social and emotional benefits that lead to successful later engagement in society. Since the publication of this report, Arts Council England launched its 'Cultural Education Challenge' and is setting up a national network of partnerships that aim to guarantee cultural experiences for every child from age five upwards, with indications that this will be extended soon to the birth-to-five age group (Arts Council England, 2015).

The Open Sesame projects take inspiration from the work of Lorenzo Malaguzzi in Reggio Emilia (Edwards et al., 1993), from UK-based projects like 5×5×5 which paired five nurseries with five artists and five galleries (Bancroft et al., 2008) and from the emerging trend for theatre companies to make new work for under-five audiences that is sensory, playful and centred on children's experience of the world. The influential REPEY and EPPE reports highlighted the importance of 'sustained shared thinking', process-led investigation and problem-solving (Siraj-Blatchford et al., 2002; Sylva et al., 2004), but also identified gaps in practitioner skills and confidence for working in this way. The Open Sesame projects have recognised that early years practitioners need certain skills in order to work creatively with children in early years education, which include being experienced in open-ended, process-led creative play that is inventive and exploratory and does not rely on predetermined end products. This approach is echoed in artists' practice, which develops through the possibilities inherent in accidents, unexpected outcomes and collaborations that are a fundamental part of process-led work. Within their particular area of art practice, they 'think visually/musically/physically' and respond to the world through these lenses; play, experimentation and willingness to fail is a vital element of working creatively and requires a commitment to the time that it takes to develop new practice. Working in this way leads to new discoveries and continual invention of new ways of working, and this is the core of the Open Sesame approach to developing confidence in working creatively in the early years workforce. To continue to develop creativity in early years settings, there is an ongoing need for regular professional collaboration with artists to inspire and stimulate practice and to be challenged to think differently and make changes.

The first project in 2010–11 (see Crabb, 2013: 7) took place in West Sussex with funding from Creative Partnerships, and county council arts and early years services. The focus was on developing creative practice in early years settings by gaining inspiration from artists who create performance work for under-fives. In partnership with early years services at West Sussex County Council and arts sector partners, the project set up creative workshops with practitioners from Oily Cart, Theatr Iolo and Lyngo Theatre amongst others and recruited a cohort of early years practitioners, experienced artists and trainee artists. After taking part in the creative sessions, the experienced and trainee artists were paired up with nurseries and led creative sessions in settings together with their partner early years practitioner.

Feedback from this project highlighted the need for more opportunities for reflection and for linking experiences to the Early Years Foundation Stage (EYFS) and child development, and for engaging parents in their children's creative learning. Another significant aspect of the project was related to attitudes to risk, and the benefit of being supported to take a risk that was beyond one's 'comfort zone' and which could lead to more transformational learning experiences. Of course, if pushed too far, this could have exactly the opposite effect, but the value of building working relationships with artists who embrace risk as part of their day-to-day practice was identified as one of the essential components of Open Sesame.

The second Open Sesame project (2012–13) took place in West Sussex, East Sussex and Surrey, with financial support from county council early years services in all three counties, from arts and cultural services and from Arts Council England, and was again managed by Culture Shift (Crabb, 2013). Practitioners from 13 early years settings took part, nine of which were in areas of deprivation. For this project, a Level 4 module was developed in partnership with the University of Brighton to provide the opportunity for early years practitioners in the project to reflect on their experiences and relate them to pedagogy and practice in the early years. The team of lead artists from the first project had set up as a company called Octopus Inc and were contracted to lead the creative programme in the project, devising a series of 'creative practice' sessions that early years practitioners and trainee artists would take part in together to gain inspiration for their work in settings. The way the project was structured established three clear forms of learning:

- creative practice sessions brought the whole group together, away from nursery settings, and provided the inspirational, and potentially higher risk, experiences in a safe and supportive environment;
- regular opportunities for testing new creative skills and approaches with children in the early years settings, led by early years practitioners and trainee artists working together with some support from the lead artists and an emphasis on observation, documentation and reflection;
- a university course which also provided opportunities for reflection and linked experiences to theory and knowledge. The trainee artists had a separate opportunity for reflecting on their experiences and developing their arts knowledge and practice through taking a Gold Arts Award.

To address the need for parent engagement, Octopus Inc devised a participatory event for parents and children aged two to five years called 'Sorted?' that would be taken out to each setting. In the development of 'Sorted?', Octopus Inc were careful to model an open-ended approach and to use cheap and easily available materials so that activities could be replicated at home. Nearly 400 children took part, along with nearly 300 parents and carers, and the response was overwhelmingly positive with plenty of evidence that this experience had given parents inspiration for new ways to play with their children at home.

As well as the success of 'Sorted?', the majority of early years practitioners passed the Level 4 module and two trainee artists gained their Gold Arts Awards. An unexpected outcome from the project was the establishment of a new partnership between the early years services and arts services in Surrey. As a result of their involvement in Open Sesame, they have continued to work together by setting up three of the settings that had taken part in the project as 'creative hubs'. Each hub continues to work with artists and then shares practice with around 30 local nurseries through twilight sessions. This activity is then extended by the early years service through advisory visits focused on linking activity to the Characteristics of Effective Learning in the EYFS (DfE, 2017: 10).

Having established the Open Sesame learning model, the third Open Sesame project (2014–16) shifted its focus to the birth-to-two age group and to establishing early years practice in cultural organisations like museums and galleries (Halstead, 2017). Running across two academic years, five partnerships in each year were set up between Children's Centres and cultural organisations in East Sussex, including Glyndebourne, De La Warr Pavilion, Ditchling Museum and Audio Active as well as those mentioned in the opening paragraph. The project also had ambitions to develop a training package for staff in museums and libraries around the region, and to adapt 'Sorted?' for children with additional needs. The Level 4 course ran in both years of the project, but this time both early years practitioners and staff from the cultural organisations took part together. The three case studies that follow give a flavour of the work that has taken place, and the changes in practice that have resulted.

Jerwood Gallery

Jerwood Gallery opened in Hastings in 2012 and houses its collection of Modern British art in a building designed to blend with the town's historic net huts and to echo the mathematical tiling, a traditional Sussex architectural feature (see Jerwood Gallery, no date). As an independent, not-for-profit organisation, every penny they make goes back into the running of the gallery and they therefore charge an admission fee but offer concessionary rates for local residents. The gallery is supported through a grant from the Jerwood Foundation, but receives no public subsidy for its core costs. Less than a mile away, East Hastings Children's Centre is located in an area that is amongst the 10% most deprived in the country, although the Jerwood Gallery itself lies outside this area.

Before taking part in Open Sesame, the Jerwood Gallery did not run any activities on a regular basis aimed at birth-to-twos, but did run some one-off pre-school events and workshops for children aged four and over. A year or so earlier, Culture Shift had facilitated initial meetings between the Children's Centre and the Jerwood Gallery, looking at how they might work together. This enabled the gallery to get

124 Clare Halstead

funding for a couple of events supported by the Children's Centre, but that funding had unfortunately come to an end.

At the start of the Open Sesame project, lead artist Alex Sutton-Vane, who had been paired with the Jerwood Gallery for the project, initially assumed that a new award-winning contemporary gallery exhibiting some extremely valuable artwork would be less than enthusiastic about opening its doors to birth-to-twos. The project therefore began by collaborating with the regular drop-in baby sessions at the Children's Centre. Working closely with Children's Centre staff, Alex planned six sensory-themed sessions: sound, smell, texture and touch, light and shade, jiggle and wiggle. These sessions provided a 'test-bed' and offered opportunities for feedback from parents, thereby building the confidence of the gallery's Education Coordinator in what might work at the gallery. Alex used both visual and sound 'provocations' for his sessions, which including singing and combining sounds with textures like jelly, cornflour, feathers and textured playdough and with smells such as citrus and herbs. Parents were amazed at how much the children responded, particularly to singing and sound, and regularly took home ideas to try out. Observations by early years practitioners during the sessions capture some of their impact on children:

> 'C (9 mths) was captivated by the sounds made by the artist; he concentrated intently on him before another activity took his attention.'
> 'S explored the balloon with rice inside. She maintained focus, putting it to her mouth and moving it from hand to hand, smiling throughout the experience.'
> 'O (7 mths) was captivated by the feathers. She intently watched her mum blowing the feather up into the air and responded with giggles and babbling.'
> 'H was fascinated by the lid on his sensory shaker. He spent 5 mins experimenting with the lid using a pincer grip.'

Through this process and the close collaboration between artist, early years practitioner and gallery staff, plans were made to transfer these activities to the Jerwood Gallery. When looked at in detail, there were only a couple of pieces of artwork that needed specific protection, and some of the building's restrictions also provided opportunities; for example, a low-light gallery was ideal for a light and shade session.

The main activity was set up in the learning space, with activities at set times either there or in gallery spaces, but children, parents and carers were also given the freedom to wander. Parents very much appreciated the opportunity to explore the gallery, sometimes sitting in front of a picture for a long time, and the children really enjoyed exploring the building; crawling up the stairs and looking out of the huge picture windows was interesting and an activity in itself.

Two sessions were planned for the gallery. For one 'non-messy' session, the learning space was full of different materials for sensory exploration, and for the other messy session the learning space was covered in paper – floors and walls – ready for using paint, shaving foam, bubbles and mashed potato. Volunteers would call people into the set activities from where they were around the gallery, or they could stay in the learning space and carry on playing. Families left their shoes and 'clean' clothes at the entrance and went through a 'cleaning zone' on exit.

In the year following the Open Sesame project, the Education Coordinator felt inspired to continue the good work. The Children's Centre supported her to design a heuristic play area in the stairwell space at the gallery, a space that is available to visitors at all times. The gallery was also keen to support and promote breastfeeding and obtained some breastfeeding-friendly signs through the Children's Centre. Following this, the Education Coordinator arranged a couple of *Baby Sense* sessions at the gallery, which were supported by an Early Years Practitioner. There was a charge of £3 per adult, but ten free places were allocated for families referred by the Children's Centre, with the aim of maintaining the opportunity for all kinds of families to share the provision but avoiding 'labelling'.

By January 2016 this arrangement had become a monthly *Baby Sense* session at the museum, and the gallery asked the Children's Centre for an Early Years Practitioner to support as before. Due to restructuring of the service, they were unable to allocate a practitioner but realised that this could be a great opportunity for a volunteer. The Children's Centre was able to find two volunteers for the first session and, while the gallery will continue to charge £3 per adult, the Children's Centre will still be able to allocate some free spaces for families they are working with.

The project had begun with one-and-a-half hour sessions but the gallery now condenses this into an hour and invites parents to stay as long as they like after the sessions have ended. Because of the original project and the partnership with the Children's Centre, the gallery has found that the sessions have brought in new visitors who had not visited the gallery before, with around 30 participants at their regular sessions.

> We feel confident that Baby Sense will continue to be a permanent part of our events programme. We would love to gain funding for the future to be able to offer one-off events on top of the regular sessions. We plan to continue to offer Baby Sense and tailor the sessions around exhibitions, local festivals and the changing seasons.
>
> (Gallery Education Coordinator)

Hastings Museum and Art Gallery

Hastings Museum and Art Gallery was established over 125 years ago and offers free entry for local people and visitors to the town to explore their collection of art, culture and history from around the world (see Hastings Museum and Art Gallery, no date). Owned and run by Hastings Borough Council, the museum was already running free weekly *Book Bugs* sessions offering a range of play activities on Wednesdays and Thursdays in partnership with their local Children's Centre. Both the museum and St Leonard's Children's Centre are located in an area that is amongst the 10% most deprived in the country. Their Thursday pre-school group

126 Clare Halstead

was initially set up in 2004 to target families with English as an additional language, and had retained a high percentage of these families, along with others referred by the Children's Centre.

> *The Museum has a strong family programme and tries to factor in activities for 0–2s wherever possible. We recognise the value of a whole family offer, and have first-hand experience of how these early visits continue, providing a good foundation for cultural engagement. We aim to make a visit as welcoming as possible for adults with young families, and have seen the benefits of this approach.*
>
> (Education Officer and Keeper of World Art)

The Wednesday group was involved in the Open Sesame project, and two members of staff from the Children's Centre were partnered with a local freelance artist who worked on behalf of the museum.

All the project sessions took place at the museum. With the support of the early years practitioners, lead artist Jenny Staff was gradually able to replace the resources that the group usually used by bringing different materials into the museum that created a series of 'provocations', changed the environment and offered different opportunities for exploration and sensory stimulation. For example, she used cardboard boxes of different sizes with various openings, hiding books and musical instruments or wrapping them in different textured fabrics, which supported children's schemas such as enveloping and transporting.

The early years practitioners and cultural partners in the project were following a module at the University of Brighton as part of the project to relate their practical learning to a theoretical context. This had ignited the passion of the early years practitioner from the Children's Centre as the changes that she and the artist were introducing to the museum sessions gave a practical context for applying Froebel's ideas about using simplified forms – cubes, spheres, cylinders – and demonstrating to parents how they are all easily accessible and found at home.

The group activities had been centred on using books and stories, but Jenny changed this focus by encouraging the parents to explore the museum collections, choosing materials that complemented their finds, and re-thinking the use of restricted spaces by creating temporary 'zones' and making better use of furniture and objects that were already there. The project allowed the group to set up zones of activity all around the top floor where the group was based and thus encouraged parents to follow their mobile children around the space; it had been ambiguous before as to how the whole space was to be used. The artist created areas of activity that related to the different exhibits in that zone and experimented with them to see what worked. This gave a clear direction and permission for children to explore and move and for parents to follow and feel comfortable.

Through the change of focus brought about by the Open Sesame sessions, the name of the group was changed to *Museum Explorers*, which more accurately reflected the emphasis on exploration and the age of the children attending and

A creative and cultural perspective **127**

which might encourage parents into the museum who may have found the *Book Bugs* name intimidating.

Parents' and practitioners' observations from the sessions about the children's responses clearly show their impact on parents' thinking about play, for example:

> *I have bought some fabric with sequins as a consequence of last week's session; J is fascinated by it and becomes very vocal when he looks at it – he reaches and grabs it and pulls it to his face*

(Parent)

> *A's (15 mths) mum said she 'has discovered that he is fascinated by opening and shutting things; and how things work'.*

(Early years practitioner observation)

The fresh approaches that the artist brought to the project provided the opportunity for significant change and, with the early years practitioners' support, expertise and knowledge, this took place without negative effects on participation.

Restructuring of Children's Centre services in East Sussex led to the cessation of support for both of the pre-school groups at the museum from April 2016. In the short term the museum continued to run the free Thursday group in partnership with a local Community Interest Company, adapting delivery to bring in some of the approaches and activities developed through Open Sesame. Sessions take themes from the museum collection and offer stories and activities to link them together and encourage parents and children to go out and about interacting with objects in a way that they did not before. However, sustaining any pre-school activity for the longer term will require external funding.

> *This is a big disappointment to the Museum and the families, as I feel that offering general groups provides a supportive way for targeted families to integrate with other activities and public programmes, developing confidence and providing opportunities for them without labels.*

(Education Officer and Keeper of World Art)

The Towner Gallery

The Towner Gallery is an independent charitable trust, which is funded by Eastbourne Borough Council and receives regular funding from Arts Council England as part of their national portfolio (see Towner Art Gallery, no date). Entry to the gallery is free, with charges made for some exhibitions and events. The gallery holds a collection of art by local, national and international artists as well as a year-round exhibition programme of contemporary and historical art, including work by local artists and schools. The Devonshire Children's Centre is located a 20-minute walk away, in the town centre Devonshire ward, which is in the 10% most deprived wards in England.

FIGURE 10.1 Explorer Jacket

Photograph reproduced with the permission of Explorer Jacket creator Jane Gordon: www.wirralsewingshed.co.uk.

Before the start of the Open Sesame project, the gallery had started to develop its work with under-fives with monthly *Tiny Towner* sessions run in partnership with Eastbourne Library and charged at £3 per child. The gallery had also commissioned artist Jane Gordon to make 'Explorer Jackets' that children aged two to five years could use when visiting the gallery (see Figure 10.1). The gallery and the Children's Centre took part in Years 1 and 2 of the Open Sesame project, with different staff and volunteers participating in each year. In the first year, the partnership was supported by lead artist Anne Colvin who specialises in dance and movement, and in the second year by visual artist Jenny Staff.

A weekly Tuesday morning drop-in aimed at birth-to-fives had been initiated shortly before joining Open Sesame, and this was a focus for development, as was the drop-in session for babies at the Children's Centre. The project sessions were split between both venues. Taking time to observe and reflect in the

A creative and cultural perspective **129**

sessions, including recording what they were seeing in real time, the group used their notes to facilitate later reflection and adapted their approaches accordingly.

Being introduced to new materials and approaches led to new activities, such as using music, movement and fabrics. By the end of the first year, the small space used for the drop-in at the gallery had been completely re-thought; for example, everyone was asked to take their shoes off before coming in and encouraged to be on the floor, making a safer and more child-centred environment. A sensory tent was commissioned from Jane Gordon and became an interactive centerpiece for the session.

Towards the end of the first year of the project, the gallery staff had built relationships with the families who began to make visits to the gallery, most for the first time. As well as these families, numbers taking part in the drop-in were increasing, leading to consideration of other changes at the gallery such as making space for buggies and introducing more high chairs and options for children in the café.

The expertise that the gallery's member of staff and volunteer built up during the first year of the project meant that they became confident in running the weekly drop-in sessions. They also encouraged the gallery to run a 'Tiny Towner Takeover Day' as part of the annual 'Takeover Day' initiative led by Kids in Museums (see Kids in Museums, 2016), and the response from families to this exceeded all expectations.

In Year 2 there was an ambition to work in the gallery spaces as well as the room that was used for the drop-in session. Another member of staff and volunteer from the gallery partnered with two different members of staff from the Children's Centre, with the potential for building new relationships. Partnership working between the gallery and the Children's Centre was affected during this year by the restructuring of Children's Centres, but by April 2016 nearly 30 families had made a visit to the gallery, and taken part in activities in one of the exhibitions.

Their comments on this experience included

- *'Thank you for such a fun morning! We really enjoyed visiting the gallery — a first for me. Staff were welcoming, friendly and very helpful. We really liked the different materials to explore. It was nice to feel comfortable in the gallery singing with my daughter. We would like to come again soon!'*
- *'Really enjoyed quiet space to play and explore while other babies were downstairs! Time slot is good too as often we can't go to groups due to my schedule. Polite and engaging staff/volunteers! Play opportunities I had not thought of (rice in balloons and space blankets) which have given me lots of creative ideas for play with both my children at home. Thank you for a lovely morning!'*
- *'I think using this as a group venue is an excellent idea. It's somewhere I wouldn't normally come, so it would encourage me to return regularly and support the Towner.'*

Reflection on the Open Sesame birth-to-twos project

Artists can find it difficult to fit into the prescribed requirements of outcomes-orientated training programmes; it is hard to evidence and measure work that is by its nature unique. The Open Sesame project, however, demonstrates a replicable model of what can be achieved through collaborative partnerships that respond to specific contexts and that achieve change through sustained and supportive relationships. There are a small number of similar projects in the UK, for example the Starcatchers project in Scotland (see Starcatchers, no date), as well as the well-known 'atelierista' model from Reggio Emilia (Edwards et al., 1993). Bringing leading galleries, museums and other cultural organisations into the original Open Sesame project adds another dimension to the idea of working with artists. This project has also been about working with cultural spaces where artists' work is being exhibited, showing how they can provide stimulation for activity and open up new spaces that are welcoming to parents and carers with babies and young children (see Figure 10.2).

FIGURE 10.2 Activities in the art gallery

Images reproduced with the permission of Culture Shift.

The transformations achieved by the Open Sesame project can be partly attributed to the quality of the relationships developed over time. Over a six- to nine-month period, the project participants had the opportunity to develop trust, both in the lead artists who are supporting them to take risks and experiment and in the partners with whom they were paired. Understanding the professional environment of someone employed in a gallery or museum takes time, and equally it takes time for someone from a gallery or museum environment to understand the day-to-day practice in a Children's Centre and the skills of the practitioners that they are working with. There are barriers to overcome, including the use of professional 'jargon' and terminology, and differences in assumptions made about the needs of children and families and the purpose of working creatively in different learning environments. There are different skill sets and knowledge, for example knowledge of art practices and historical artefacts, or of language and communication and child development. At times, some early years practitioners felt that they were having to fill in a lot of early years knowledge that cultural participants did not have, as some had never worked with this age group before and did not have knowledge of the EYFS. However, having time to understand each other's skills and knowledge meant that the differences between participants increased the diversity of experience in the project overall, rather than acting as a barrier. Although the project encouraged all the participants to develop confidence in their own creativity, the intention was not that all the participants would be able to take on the role of the artist by the end of the project. While everyone can be creative, not everyone is an artist and this is a distinction that helps to illuminate the particular skills of professional artists.

Through the six creative practice sessions spread out over that period, and the ongoing support from a lead artist assigned to each partnership, the participants developed trust in the creative process of the project. The lead artists encouraged the participants to play, and through playing with materials to notice their own and others' sensory responses, and to interact playfully with each other. Reflection was built into this process so that experiences were discussed and recorded and their potential for use in sessions with children and families was explored. The enjoyment and playfulness of these sessions helped the participants to bond and, by involving them in process-led exploratory play, develop confidence in this way of working which they could then model in sessions with children and families. The creative practice sessions included more unfamiliar art-forms such as dance and sound, and by the end of the project, all the participants reported increased confidence in using a range of art-forms with birth-to-twos and families.

The length of the project also gave the participants time to develop and test their ideas. The iterative process moved the participants around the different contexts of Children's Centre groups, gallery and museum spaces, creative practice sessions and university sessions, allowing ideas to cross-fertilise gradually, and providing regular opportunities to test ideas in practical situations. Changes in practice were therefore based on experimentation and testing, including feedback from observations of children and conversations with parents, and the introduction of new ways of working were achieved with the support of managers in both early years and cultural settings. Time was also essential for forging relationships with families. Cultural partners visiting the sessions at Children's Centres were gradually able to establish positive relationships with children and their parents and carers, but it took some time for this to be strong enough to encourage them to visit for the first time.

The quality of the practitioners, including the lead artists, the early years practitioners, the gallery staff and the university course leader also contributed to the success of the project. The lead artists had had the experience of the two previous projects to draw on, as well as being individually experienced in using their art practice in early years. The university course added value to the learning process through linking the participants' experiences with theories of child development and pedagogy. For some early years practitioners this meant re-visiting some previous areas of study but, with the added context of a live project environment, this was productive and encouraged them to push their practice further. For some of the cultural participants, this was the first time they had engaged in this area of study and the module was an essential adjunct to their learning in the rest of the project, providing a theoretical base for the work. The whole group kept reflective journals during the project and all found this an extremely valuable part of the process.

As well as staff and volunteers directly involved in the project, there must also be mention of the managers and wider teams of staff and volunteers that supported the project. The time that had to be committed to the project meant time away from other aspects of people's roles but in each partnership this time was found. New initiatives or changes to ways of working also meant that there were impacts on others; for example, in galleries and museums that were not used to welcoming very young children there were questions to answer about the practicalities of the work and impacts on other visitors, and mitigating these impacts is once again a positive feature of a project that develops progressively over a number of months as there is time to work through these questions.

The Open Sesame project has shown how working with the very youngest has brought families who are not regular gallery and museum visitors into these spaces for the first time, and given them very positive experiences. Arts and cultural organisations face an ongoing challenge in attracting audiences who are not regular arts attenders, and who are from more deprived socio-economic areas, and a successful first visit by these audiences is crucial in retaining them. However, as has also been learnt through the Open Sesame project, successful partnership working with early years provision in the wider community has been a crucial ingredient in making these experiences successful. The current re-organisation of early years services threatens these partnerships for the future as professional early years staff are increasingly focused on working with the most needy families instead of supporting universal provision, so the availability of staff to participate in future Open Sesame-type projects could be severely limited. However, the re-organisation of services for early intervention also includes more thinking about integrated

A creative and cultural perspective **133**

working across services (see for example, Messenger and Molloy, 2014) and, if the arts and cultural sector were to be included in these developments, then partnership working could be enhanced in the future. The arts and cultural sector is certainly thinking this way, with initiatives around Cultural Commissioning and the setting up of the national network of Cultural Education Partnerships (National Council for Voluntary Organisations, 2017). Opening up cultural spaces in museums, galleries, libraries and theatres to the very youngest children and their families would seem to be one of the most valuable contributions that the cultural sector can make to children's development, to social cohesion and to establishing life-long engagement in culture. Open Sesame shows how this can be achieved through collaboration between artists, arts organisations and early years services – it just needs some creative thinking.

Questions

Thinking of your local museum or art gallery, what does it offer to families with very young children? How does it attract audiences who are not regular arts attenders or who are from more deprived socio-economic areas?

What do you think artists bring to working creatively with young children that early years educators don't?

Further reading

Hannah, W. (2014). A Reggio-inspired music atelier: Opening the door between visual arts and music. *Early Childhood Education Journal*, 42, 287–294.

This article explores how a Reggio-inspired atelier (art studio) can be expanded to include music. Commonalities between visual art and music are discussed, as well as the use of music learning techniques, materials, and documentation for the music atelier. Because both music and art are non-verbal languages, musical activities in the atelier 'are meant to express a child's perspective, feelings, ideas and imagination' (p. 293).

References and useful websites

Arts Council England (2015). *The Cultural Education Challenge*. Available at www.artscouncil.org. uk/children-and-young-people/cultural-education-challenge (Accessed on: 22/01/2017).

Bancroft, S., Fawcett, M. and Hay P. (eds.) (2008). *Researching Children Researching the World: 5×5×5=creativity*. Stoke on Trent: Trentham Books.

Crabb, N. (2013). *Exploring Together: Open Sesame Project Evaluation Report*. Available at www.cultureshift.org.uk/wp-content/uploads/2012/10/OpenSesame_Report_LZ.pdf (Accessed on: 22/01/2017).

Culture Shift (no date). *Open Sesame*. Available at www.cultureshift.org.uk/what-we-do/open-sesame (Accessed on: 22/01/2017).

Department for Education (DfE) (2017). *Statutory Framework for the Early Years Foundation Stage*. Available at www.foundationyears.org.uk/eyfs-statutory-framework/ (Accessed on: 27/07/2017).

134 Clare Halstead

Doeser, J. (2015). *Step by Step: Arts Policy and Young People 1944–2014.* London: Kings College London. Available at www.kcl.ac.uk/cultural/culturalenquiries/youngpeople/Step-by-step.pdf (Accessed on: 22/01/2017).

Edwards, C., Gandini, L., and Forman, G. (eds.) (1993). *The Hundred Languages of Children: The Reggio Emilia Approach to Early Childhood Education.* Norwood, NJ: Ablex.

Halstead, C. (2017). *Open Sesame: Unlocking Creativity in Early Years 2010–2016.* Culture Shift. Available at www.cultureshift.org.uk/wp-content/uploads/2014/12/OpenSesame_Evaluation_FINAL.pdf (Accessed on: 22/01/2017).

Hastings Museum and Art Gallery (no date). *About the Museum.* Available at www.hmag.org.uk/aboutus/about/ (Accessed on: 22/01/2017).

Jerwood Gallery (no date). *The Gallery.* Available at www.jerwoodgallery.org/about/the-gallery (Accessed on: 22/01/2017).

Kids in Museums (2016). *Takeover Day England.* Available at http://kidsinmuseums.org.uk/takeoverday/ (Accessed on: 22/01/2017).

Messenger, C. and Molloy, D. (2014). *Getting it Right for Families: A Review of Integrated Systems and Promising Practice in the Early Years.* Available at www.eif.org.uk/wp-content/uploads/2014/11/GETTING-IT-RIGHT-FULL-REPORT.pdf (Accessed on: 22/01/2017).

National Council for Voluntary Organisations (2017). *Cultural Commissioning Programme.* Available at www.ncvo.org.uk/practical-support/public-services/cultural-commissioning-programme (Accessed on: 22/01/2017).

Siraj-Blatchford, I., Sylva, K., Muttock. S., Gilden, R., and Bell, D. (2002). *Researching Effective Pedagogy in the Early Years.* DfES Research Report 365. London: HMSO.

Starcatchers (no date). *Who We Are.* Available at www.starcatchers.org.uk/who-we-are/ (Accessed on: 22/01/2017).

Sylva, K., Melhuish, E. C., Sammons, P., Siraj-Blatchford, I., and Taggart, B. (2004). *The Effective Provision of Pre-school Education (EPPE) Project. Technical Paper 12: Final Report – Effective Pre-school Education.* London: DfES/University of London Institute of Education.

Towner Art Gallery (no date). *About Towner.* Available at www.townereastbourne.org.uk/about-towner/ (Accessed on: 22/01/2017).

University of Manchester (no date). *The Whitworth: Early Years.* Available at www.whitworth.manchester.ac.uk/learn/earlyyears/ (Accessed on: 22/01/2017).

11

WORKING WITH TWO-YEAR-OLDS

The role of Educational Psychologist

Anita Soni

Introduction

As noted in Chapters 7 and 8, the funded places for two-year-olds initiative brought practitioners into contact with children and families who had perhaps more complex needs than they had previously experienced, and as a consequence settings found they needed help and guidance from external agencies. This includes working with Educational Psychologists – and I am fortunate to work as an Educational Psychologist. This chapter will briefly discuss five aspects of our work – assessment; consultation and intervention; evidence-based practice; supervision; and training – that have relevance for work with two-year-olds, their parents/carers and practitioners.

Assessment

An Educational Psychologist's role spans work with children from birth to the age of 25 years in educational and early years settings. The definition below highlights the potential role of Educational Psychologists (EPs) in early years, although the role tends to be associated more with schools:

> Educational psychologists tackle challenges such as learning difficulties, social and emotional problems, issues around disability as well as more complex developmental disorders. Local authorities employ the majority of educational psychologists. A growing number work as independent or private consultants.
>
> (BPS, 2013:1)

As indicated in the definition, the role also can become focused on children with special educational needs and disabilities (SEND) and this is reinforced by the statutory duties of EPs employed by a Local Authority as outlined in the DfE/DoH

136 Anita Soni

(2015) Special Educational Needs and Disability (SEND) Code of Practice: 0–25 years. This gives statutory guidance for organisations which work with and support children and young people who have special educational needs or disabilities.

In seeking advice and information, the local authority should consider with professionals what advice they can contribute to ensure the assessment covers all the relevant education, health and care needs of the child or young person. Advice and information **must** be sought as follows:

- Advice and information from the child's parent or the young person. The local authority **must** take into account his or her views, wishes and feelings.
- Educational advice and information from a person responsible for educational provision for the child or young person.
- Medical advice and information from health care professionals with a role in relation to the child's or young person's health.
- Psychological advice and information from an educational psychologist who should normally be employed or commissioned by the local authority. The educational psychologist should consult any other psychologists known to be involved with the child or young person.
- Social care advice and information from or on behalf of the local authority, including, if appropriate, children in need or child protection assessments, information from a looked after child's care plan, or adult social care assessments for young people over 18.

(DfE/DoH, 2015: 156–157)

The statutory duties for an EP are central, and the psychological advice and information that contributes towards the assessment for an Education, Health and Care Plan are important, but there is a danger this can become the only role EPs undertake in early years settings. However, before considering other aspects of the role within early years, it is helpful to consider assessment from an EP's perspective.

The assessment role is critical and frequently means working within short time frames as advice has to be given within six weeks of the request or quicker than this where possible (DfE/DoH, 2015). Therefore, the process relies on getting high-quality assessment information from those most closely involved with the child. In terms of two-year-olds, this will tend to be gained in the following ways:

- observations of the child in their home and early years settings;
- interviews with key adults in the child's life such as the child's parents and Key Person;
- reviewing assessment information available on the child. This could include looking at the child's red book or other health records, curriculum-based assessments in the form of Learning Journeys and Portage assessments and reports;

The role of Educational Psychologist **137**

- reviewing additional forms of assessment/information such as Early Help assessments or Child in Need or Child Protection plans.

In terms of what is most important as an external professional, essentially it is quality, rather than quantity that is key. The best observations are those that show the child doing what they enjoy, at their most relaxed and comfortable, in a range of contexts. If the EP is faced with a lot of repetitive information, or information that is badly organised, or very sparse, this can be difficult to make sense of, and does not give a rounded picture of the child, including their strengths and areas of difficulty. This type of work is considered to be direct work with children, as the EP is assessing the child, and looking at progress over time. In addition, EPs may use standardised tests with the child, although with two-year-olds, this is less likely than with a school-aged child. It may involve an assessment similar to that undertaken by a Health Visitor such as the Schedule of Growing Skills (SOGS) or a standardised checklist such as the Parental Involvement Project (PIP) developmental charts (Jeffree and McConkey, 1998), or a dynamic assessment whereby the EP observes how the child responds to different play activities and experiences.

Consultation and intervention

EPs also work within a consultation approach. This may involve working directly with a child, as detailed previously, but might also focus on working with the key adults in the child's life to offer support and advice. The adult seeking support is considered to be the expert on the child, so sometimes EPs may not observe the child, but seek to use their psychological knowledge alongside the adult's in-depth knowledge of the child, to discuss and reflect on different ideas and strategies, using problem-solving approaches. An example of this type of work with young children is working collaboratively with a Key Person to identify ways to support the child with his or her communication and/or behaviour. As an EP, I am frequently asked about a child's behaviour, and the first step towards resolving any difficulties is seeking to understand the child's behaviour and how this relates to the child's communication with others, their relationships, their environment and their stage of development.

Sally asked to discuss Oliver, a young child she is working with who can bite others. This tends to be focused on one or two children. Sally had already undertaken some ABC (antecedent – behaviour – consequence) observations and found biting happens at different times of the day, and so there didn't seem to be a pattern. We discussed Sally doing some observations of Oliver to see not only when he engages in biting, but why, and what his biting might be communicating. Sally also agreed to talk to Oliver's parents about the biting to see if he was also doing the same at home.

Sally started to notice that Oliver is biting the children in his key group and that one occasion he was about to bite Janice, the new early years practitioner, who has recently started working in the room. Sally identified that Oliver was excited when he bit others, and that he showed an ability to stop the bite with adults when reminded. Sally found out that Oliver has been biting before at home but only occasionally, and again it seemed to be when he was being very affectionate towards his Dad. Sally and I talked about creating and re-inforcing a behaviour that Oliver could display to help him show his affection and excitement in a more acceptable way, and it was agreed to help him by encouraging him (and all the other children) to give high fives.

Evidence-based practice

In addition to this more familiar role, EPs take an evidence-based approach to their work and, as the BPS identifies:

> research innovative ways of helping vulnerable young people and often train teachers, learning support assistants and others working with children.
>
> (BPS, 2013: 1)

An example of evidence-based work relating to supporting parents with their two-year-olds at home or practitioners in early years settings that EPs, amongst other professionals, may utilise is Video Interactive Guidance™. This is an intervention through which a trained guider uses video clips to improve communication within the relationship being recorded (Association for Video Interactive Guidance UK [AVIG UK], 2016). It is vital that the client, in this case a parent or a practitioner, is happy to have a video recording taken, and identifies a helping question which relates to an aspect of their relationship with their child which they would like to develop. Video Interactive Guidance™ builds on the central ideas of Trevarthen in relation to primary and secondary intersubjectivity and mediated learning as discussed in Chapters 2 and 3. The guider works alongside the client to examine short sections of video where the parent has demonstrated the principles of attunement to their child (AVIG UK, 2016).

I have been using the approach of Video Interactive Guidance with Sarah, who wants to develop her communication and relationships with her youngest child. Initially we started by looking at a video of her playing with her older child, Gemma, but this quickly moved to Sarah considering her younger child, Frankie, whom she has identified as having difficulties with attention, and who is less likely to play with Sarah or her older sister Gemma. Sarah and I undertook a second round of Video Interactive Guidance looking at her interaction with Frankie, before moving on to supporting Sarah to be with both of her children at the same time.

Supervision

Supervision is an aspect of professional practice that I was unfamiliar with when I worked as a teacher, but is an essential part of practice for EPs. The Health and Care Professions Council (HCPC) highlights the central importance of supervision within the Standards of Proficiency for Practitioner Psychologists in order to 'be able to practise as an autonomous professional, exercising their own professional judgement' (HCPC, 2015: 8).

Similarly, the BPS identify supervision as a duty with the ethical principle of competence (BPS, 2009), in order to work at the optimal level whilst recognising the limits of understanding, skills, training and experience, and that supervision is needed to ensure ethical decision-making.

The Statutory Framework for the Early Years Foundation Stage (EYFS) (DfE, 2014) included supervision for the first time as an entitlement for those who have contact with children and their families. The EYFS promotes a child-centred approach to supervision, and identifies that supervision should provide support, opportunities for problem-solving, confidential discussion of sensitive issues, coaching and training. Dunsmuir and Leadbetter (2010) highlight that EPs are frequently commissioned to provide supervision to other professional groups and give examples from early years services such as Family Support Workers in Children's Centres and Portage home visitors. This experience of delivering supervision indicates that EPs could provide supervision to other professional groups within early years.

> I offer group supervision to a group of managers who work across a group of nurseries run by a board of trustees. This regular supervision is bound by a contract identifying the purposes of the supervision, who attends, how records of the sessions will be kept, frequency of meetings, scope, issues of confidentiality and evaluation. This gives protected time to enable managers to get their own supervision, work collaboratively, reflect on their work, and engage in problem-solving over issues that arise as well as share successes and plan forward steps for the organisation.

Training

Training is also an area where EPs can support those working in early years provision. This could relate to a number of issues including SEND, child development, observation and assessment amongst other issues related to psychology such as the Key Person approach. This is an opportunity to work across the workforce rather than with one child, or one Key Person or parent, and so gives a greater opportunity for impact.

> I have been asked to deliver a short evening training session on supervision by a Local Authority training officer. The training gives an opportunity to reflect on models, theories and practice in supervision from other professions, as well as considering and rehearsing the skills needed, through role play and watching video clips, alongside the practical issues of policies and contracts.

I hope this gives a flavour of the type of work that is undertaken by EPs who work with two-year-olds, and so offers a different perspective on the figured world of the early years setting.

Questions

Thinking about supervision, what advantages and disadvantages can you see in being supervised by someone who does not work in your setting?

Use of video clips is becoming a familiar feature in research, professional development and parenting interventions. Can you anticipate any difficulties with this technique? What are the advantages – and what alternatives could be employed?

Further reading

Soni, A. (2013). Group supervision: Supporting practitioners in their work with children and families in Children's Centres. *Early Years* 33(2), 146–160.

This article is based on research with four Children's Centres, which evaluated group supervision with Family Support Workers and centre managers. With a view to understanding how group supervision can support the continuing professional development of those working with children and families in early years provision in England, key mechanisms and contextual features are identified within the group supervision process.

References

Association of Video Interaction Guidance UK (AVIG UK) (2016). *About VIG*. Available at www.videointeractionguidance.net/aboutvig (Accessed on: 04/04/2016).

British Psychological Society (BPS) (2009). *Code of Ethics and Conduct*, Leicester: British Psychological Society.

British Psychological Society (BPS) (2013). *Careers – Educational Psychology*. Available at http://careers.bps.org.uk/area/educational (Accessed on: 02/04/2016).

Department for Education (DfE) (2014). *Statutory Framework for the Early Years Foundation Stage*. Available at www.foundationyears.org.uk/eyfs-statutory-framework/ (Accessed on: 27/07/2017).

Department for Education/Department of Health (DfE/DoH) (2015). *Special Educational Needs and Disability (SEND) Code of Practice: 0–25 Years*. Available at www.gov.uk/government/uploads/system/uploads/attachment_data/file/398815/SEND_Code_of_Practice_January_2015.pdf (Accessed on: 02/04/2016).

Dunsmuir, S. and Leadbetter, J. (2010). *Professional Supervision: Guidelines for Practice for Educational Psychologists*, Leicester: Division of Educational and Child Psychology (DECP) and British Psychological Society (BPS).

Health and Care Professionals Council (HCPC) (2015). *Practitioner Psychologists: Standards of Proficiency*, London: HCPC.

Jeffree, D. M. and McConkey, R. (1998). *PIP Developmental Charts*, London: Hodder Education.

12

CONCLUDING THOUGHTS

What matters for high-quality experiences for two-year-olds in early years settings?

Carmen Dalli

This book has been written with a particular group of early years practitioners in mind: those who work with two-year-olds across a wide range of early years settings. Its intention has been to bring together theoretical and practical insights from research to provide professional support and inspiration to practitioners aiming to create high-quality pedagogical contexts for two-year-olds and their families.

That the book is timely is undeniable. OECD (2016) figures show that between 2006 and 2014 the participation rates for children from birth to two years of age in formal childcare and preschool[1] services increased by an average of five percentage points across 30 of its 38 member countries.[2] Within this, there are some big variations by country. For example, while New Zealand participation rates for children from birth to two years of age increased in line with the OECD average (5%), Germany and Korea had percentage growth rates as high as 18.7% and 24.5%. In the UK, by contrast, there was a drop in participation rates for children aged from birth to two years between 2006 and 2014[3] though the overall participation rate was still the same as for the average in the OECD: 35%. Overall, it is clear that now, as never before, very young children are experiencing their childhood in a very different way to previous generations.

The chapters of this book have engaged critically with a range of topics that have provided a broad context for the new global phenomenon of group-based early childhood services for children of a very young age, and sought to answer the question of how – in this new normality of children's lives – it might be possible for contemporary societies to ensure a good childhood for their very youngest citizens.

In this concluding chapter, my task is to highlight some overarching messages from the chapters and to address the question: what matters to ensure high-quality experiences for two-year-olds in early years settings?

While acknowledging the impossibility of capturing every nuanced argument in the book and the rich discussion in each chapter – including debates on the many

Concateng thoughts **143**

ways that 'quality' and 'good childhood' might be understood – I want to focus on three key messages, chief among which is the first: two-year-olds in group-based early years settings thrive in relationships with knowledgeable and responsive practitioners. Secondly, structural elements of the environment matter, including regulable elements of quality – such as adult-to-child ratios – since these provide pre-conditions for other characteristics of quality experiences. Thirdly, a supportive policy infrastructure matters if an ongoing culture of quality provision is to be achieved.

Relationships with knowledgeable, responsive practitioners

It matters that very young children experience responsive relationships with the practitioners with whom they spend many hours of their day. As both Rod Parker Rees and Gill Boag-Munroe show in Chapters 2 and 5, two-year-olds pay close attention to the way other people respond to them and to things and events around them; this helps them 'harvest' the cultural information they need to become expert participants in their community. Adults' responses to children – through language in all its forms – also construct children's identities, with potentially lifelong implications for how children view themselves. Within early years settings, this means that children do not just need any relationship with any adult. Rather, it matters that children have a relationship with practitioners who are knowledgeable about their role and its inherent power to shape lives.

Knowledgeable practitioners understand children and their development; they know about, and are skilled at, reading the subtle cues that very young children give, including about their temperament and age characteristics. Although infants and toddlers may not express themselves articulately in language, research continues to clarify that even very young children have elaborate communicative competences whose meaning can be understood by an attentive or 'watchful' and responsive adult (see Chapters 4 and 6). For example, we know a lot more about the complex meanings that under-one-year-olds can convey through gestures (Crais et al., 2009), and how babies pay more attention to dynamic new faces and learn them faster than static images (Valenza et al., 2015). This parallels the way in which they follow someone else's gaze when they are interested in what that person is attending to.

Our increased understanding about very young children's competences makes it imperative that when working with infants and toddlers, early years practitioners have the knowledge to recognise their competences and respond to them. In particular, it has been shown that for under-two-year-olds, 'serve-and-return' interactions with adults promote reciprocity in interaction and create intersubjective attunement (National Scientific Council on the Developing Child, 2004). These interactions are like a ping-pong or table tennis exchange – you serve the ball and wait for it to be returned, and the way you serve it back depends on how it has been returned to you. In other words, the adult here makes the child's contribution to the exchange the focus of their response. When an infant's vocalisations are welcomed and responded to in this way, the child will learn to vocalise more. Children learn from the adult's response that their vocalisations produce a result. If the adult's response is appropriate, and shows awareness of the child's needs, a feeling of close emotional attachment grows between the child and the adult. As outlined also by Anita Soni in Chapter 3, close emotional attachments with adults provide a secure base for children. Children will seek out those adults when they need comfort, or when they are uncertain how to react in a new situation. In such attachment relationships, children learn about trust, reciprocity in communication, and care: These are all elements of well-functioning interpersonal relationships at any stage of life.

Across a number of chapters, it is clear that current pedagogical research about working with infants and toddlers is giving great attention to the psychological concepts of reciprocity, sensitive responsiveness, and intersubjectivity. When these concepts are enacted, the adult typically takes on many roles vis-à-vis the child: an attachment figure, a partner in a relational dance, a mediator who opens up the world to the child (Edwards and Raikes, 2002; Johansson, 2004) in an intentional expression of care (Mitchelmore et al., 2017).

In the early years, learning is primarily about children acquiring a sense of identity, gaining language, and a sense that they belong and can contribute; that they are worthy of attention. These learning outcomes, or dimensions of being human, are interactive and learned in social settings within a culture (Rogoff et al., 2014). They are not innate; these lessons are learned within relationships where there is sensitive responsive caregiving. Neurobiological research is increasingly showing that this kind of caregiving is the key environmental factor needed for optimal brain development: it wires up the brain for learning and leads to emotion regulation (Campos et al., 2004). By contrast, lack of attuned responsive caregiving constrains the developing brain, creating 'black holes' in the architecture of the brain that can persist throughout a lifetime (Turp, 2006: 306).

So, it matters that children encounter adults in early years settings who are knowledgeable about the kinds of interactions that children thrive on, and can engage in these interactions effectively and with sensitivity. In Chapter 6, Jan Georgeson describes how this knowledge can be enacted in practice through the use of the terms 'anticipatory watchfulness', 'relational anticipation' and 'pedagogical tact'. Each serves to remind us of the essential place that intersubjectivity – the ability to establish joint attention and shared meaning – has in pedagogy with this age group. Such pedagogical skills matter particularly when the educator or practitioner is just getting to know a new child – of whatever age – but especially infants and two-year-olds.

It also matters that the teachers are knowledgeable about building relationships with the families who entrust their precious child to them. For families, starting to use an early years setting for their child is never easy. The phenomenon of maternal separation anxiety has long been documented (e.g., Hock et al., 1989). In my own research, I found that when settling in their child, parents were inevitably beset by fears for the child, and worries about whether they were doing the right thing; guilt was never far below the surface (Dalli, 1999). Traditional images of 'ideal motherhood', sitting at home surrounded with beautifully behaved happy

Concluding thoughts **145**

children, still haunt many women as they make the decision to go back to work. Could they trust the adults at the nursery to offer the best that they themselves could offer? What happens when they're not there? Was their child old enough or ready for preschool? What if she got hurt? Would their child be looked after or ignored? And they wanted to keep on side with the practitioner in order not to give her a reason to 'not like my child'. There were many hidden power issues at play. What the mothers desperately wanted was evidence that their child would be well looked after – loved even – but what then if the child ended up loving the teacher more than them? This complex array of emotions is very hard on parents and, while the memory of them fades in intensity with the passage of time, they are very difficult to navigate at the time.

So it matters that teachers are knowledgeable about how parents feel and can draw on strategies that can reassure parents. This starts to build the basis for a collaborative and supportive relationship and a sense of partnership.

A strategy that can help is the establishment of a primary caregiving, or key person, system. As Anita Soni alludes to in Chapter 3, the essence of a key person system is that each child has one practitioner who has primary responsibility for building a relationship with them and their family from the moment the child is enrolled. In this way, the practitioner can ask about the child's routine at home; about the child's bodily rhythms and temperament; how the home adults hold their baby when they give them a bottle; how they settle them to sleep in a cot; do they have any special toys that comfort them? In gaining this information, the practitioner can gauge how the parents feel about the experience of starting to use an early years setting and thus adjust their response to be the most helpful possible. Having a primary caregiver or key person does not mean that the child and family will not interact with other adults in the setting; to function well the system needs each child to also have a back-up person who likewise keeps an eye on the child and can step in if the primary caregiver cannot be there. And it also needs all staff in the setting to be fully committed to making the system work (Dalli and Kibble, 2010). The benefits of having a nominated practitioner as the key contact for a family is that both child and family gain the security of knowing that 'someone is looking after me here'. As the child settles into the early years setting, the key person also encourages additional relationships with other adults in the setting, but retains the overall responsibility for that child. Regular communication with the home adults at drop-off or pick-up time, and nowadays increasingly during the day through technologies like Skype and electronic portfolios, can do a lot to take the edge off the worry. Explaining how the key person system works, and clarifying that the system is there as a support for the family, and not just for the child at the setting, can build the basis of a trusting relationship between practitioners and parents. It can allay any fears that the practitioners will supplant the parent in the child's affection.

Clearly, relationships with practitioners do matter; not just any relationship with any practitioner but an attuned responsive relationship with a knowledgeable practitioner. Knowledgeable practitioners understand the importance of interactions that are cued to the child's signals and use this knowledge as the basis of their

146 Carmen Dalli

pedagogy. They also understand the importance of working alongside parents to guide and reassure them as they handle this major transition in the life of their family.

Structural elements matter

The second key message I want to focus on is that it matters what type of environment children spend their time in. I am referring not only to the way that the spatial and material characteristics of an early years setting enable or constrain children's mobility, agency and social interactions (Pairman and Dalli, 2017) – as evident in Karen Wickett's chapter (Chapter 9) – but also to the holistic impact of the setting on children's and practitioners' well-being, including their stress levels.

Neuroscientific research over the last few decades has alerted us to the damaging effects of high stress levels on healthy brain development, and thus the need to ensure that environments for children actively avoid stress, or are able to buffer children against it. When there is continuous high stress over which the child has no control and no access to support from an adult to help soothe them, the stress becomes toxic (National Scientific Council on the Developing Child, 2004). Low-quality care, either at home or out-of-home, can give rise to toxic stress and prevent the development of a history of attuned interactions. By contrast, low-stress environments are correlated to healthy brain development because in low-stress environments, attuned care and supportive relationships are more possible.

Fortunately, we know quite a lot about how to create low-stress environments in early years settings, and most of what is needed is amenable to policy intervention through regulation of aspects such as ratios of adults to children; group size (Dalli and Pairman, 2013); staff qualifications; and building standards about space requirements to enable a range of activities, minimise noise diffusion, and allow for calm and quiet rest spaces.

Nonetheless, regulations by themselves are not sufficient. For example, we know that an adult-to-child ratio of 1:3 in two-year-old settings is considered ideal for the style of interaction that is valued in Western cultures (Gevers Deynoot-Schaub and Riksen-Walraven, 2008). But we also know that by themselves ratios do not guarantee good outcomes; they interact with other factors (Munton et al., 2002). In other words, ratios provide the pre-conditions for positive interactions, but the nature of the adult–child interactions themselves may be determined by factors such as levels of staff satisfaction, which in turn interact with factors like appropriate levels of remuneration (Goelman et al., 2006).

With regard to staff qualifications, the same dynamic applies: high levels of training – both pre-service and in-service – are associated with quality outcomes for infants and toddlers (Munton et al., 2002) but qualifications work in conjunction with a range of other variables to create a 'climate for quality' (Raikes et al., 2006: 131). For example, it has been argued that the content of the training or qualifications must be relevant to the age group and reflect what is known about infant learning and development (Elfer and Dearnley, 2007; Hallam et al., 2003;

Macfarlane et al., 2004). There is a link between higher-level qualifications and a positive attitude towards infants and toddlers and their learning (Arnett, 1989; Kowalski et al., 2005), and between inclusive practices with infants and toddlers and higher levels of teacher education and adult-to-child ratios (Hestenes et al., 2007). Mentoring of less-experienced staff by more experienced colleagues has been reported to be an effective professional development model in enhancing sensitivity to infants (Fiene, 2002). Furthermore, the inclusion of critical reflection, a focus on understanding the diversity of children's and families' contemporary lives (Macfarlane et al., 2004), and a research and evaluation focus (Nimmo and Park, 2009) in teacher preparation programmes, are associated with more reflective practitioners who are innovative in their practice.

These findings provide some clear directions for what training programmes for work with two-year-olds should, or could, look like.

A supportive policy infrastructure matters

The third key message I want to focus on is that the realisation of quality early years services for two-year-olds requires a supportive policy infrastructure that is fully resourced.

It is clear from the account provided in the introductory chapter of this book, and elsewhere in this collection, that the provision of early years services for two-year-olds within the English context is challenged by a number of factors that require policy attention. As in most countries, it is still rare to find highly qualified staff working with children up to two-years-old (see Chapter 4). Furthermore, as Verity Campbell-Barr notes in Chapter 7, most practitioners working with this age group come to know how to work with young children in other ways than through formal qualifications. Introducing this book, the editors – Verity Campbell-Barr and Jan Georgeson – argue that the historically complex models of training and the mixed economy of provision have resulted in practical problems of resourcing as well as of ensuring quality.

Elsewhere, I have argued the need for policy to act as a supportive membrane for high-quality professional practice. In the context of a retrenched early childhood policy context in New Zealand, I recently analysed the tensions and challenges experienced by early childhood teachers in seeking to enact the kind of relational pedagogy with infants and toddlers described earlier in this chapter (Dalli, 2017). I argued that relying solely on the actions of teachers working at the local level of their early childhood setting could only do so much to remedy systemic policy failure. I linked this to earlier analyses within the international *Day in the life of an early years practitioner study* where we had similarly concluded that professional practice is not the result of pedagogical action taken by one practitioner, or group of practitioners, in a setting on their own (Miller et al., 2012). Admirable and inspirational as such action can be – and this is illustrated in this book by at least Chapter 9 and Chapter 10 – to be sustainable, good-quality professional practice requires policy support both within the immediate early years setting and at the wider societal

148 Carmen Dalli

level. In other words, good-quality professional practice is an ecology that requires different elements to work together at multiple levels (see also Dalli and Urban, 2010). This then requires that policy work together with the insights from research and practice.

At the end of this highly timely book, when early years provision for two-year olds remains a priority for families but seems to have slipped off the list of active agenda items for systematic policy both in England as well as in New Zealand, this seems a message that is worth repeating.

Notes

1   Formal childcare or preschool services generally include centre-based services (e.g. nurseries or daycare centres and pre-schools, both public and private), organised family daycare, and care services provided by (paid) professional childminders – but excludes children that use unpaid services provided by relatives, friends or neighbours. Definitions of these services may vary from country to country; data collected from various statistical authorities and cross-national surveys.
2   The average participation rate for birth to two-year-olds in OECD countries was just over 34% in 2014; in UK it was appox 35% of all birth to two-year-olds.
3   The other countries with falling participation rates for birth to two-year-olds are Greece, Italy and Spain: www.oecd.org/els/soc/PF3_2_Enrolment_childcare_preschool.pdf (Accessed on: 17/09/2017).

References

Arnett, J. (1989). Caregivers in day-care centers. Does training matter? *Journal of Applied Developmental Psychology*, 10(4), 541–552.
Campos, J. J., Frankel, C. B., and Camras, L. (2004). On the nature of emotion regulation. *Child Development*, 75(2), 377–394.
Crais, E., Watson, L., and Baranek, G. (2009). Use of gesture development in profiling children's prelinguistic communication skills. *American Journal of Speech-Language Pathology*, 18(1), 95–108.
Dalli, C. (1999). Learning to be in childcare: Mothers' stories of their child's 'settling-in'. *European Early Childhood Research Journal*, 7(2), 53–66.
Dalli, C. (2017). Tensions and challenges in professional practice with under-threes: A New Zealand reflection on early childhood professionalism as a systemic phenomenon. In E. J. White and C. Dalli (eds.), *Policy and pedagogy with under-three-year olds* (pp. 115–129). Dordrecht. Springer.
Dalli, C., and Kibble, N. (2010). Peaceful caregiving as curriculum: Insights on primary caregiving from action research. In A. Meade (Ed.), *Dispersing waves: Innovation in early childhood education* (pp. 27–34). Wellington: NZCER.
Dalli, C., and Pairman, A. (2013). Group size in infant and toddler settings: Old news in a new context calls for new research. *The First Years: New Zealand Journal of Infant and Toddler Education*, 15(2), 8–16.
Dalli, C., and Urban, M. (2010). Conclusion. Towards new understandings of the early years profession: The need for a critical ecology. In C. Dalli and M. Urban (eds.), *Professionalism in early childhood education and care: International perspectives* (pp. 150–155). London and New York: Routledge.

Edwards, C., and Raikes, H. (2002). Extending the dance: Relationship-based approaches to infant/toddler care and education. *Young Children*, 57(4), 10–17.

Elfer, P., and Dearnley, K. (2007). Nurseries and emotional well-being: Evaluating an emotionally containing model of professional development. *Early Years*, 27(3), 257–279.

Fiene, R. (2002). Improving child care quality through an infant caregiver mentoring project. *Child and Youth Care Forum*, 31(2), 79–87.

Gevers Deynoot-Schaub, M. J. and Riksen-Walraven J. M. (2008). Infants in group care: Their interactions with professional caregivers and parents across the second year of life. *Infant Behavior and Development*, 31(2), 181–189.

Goelman, H. B., Forer, P., Kershaw, G., Doherty, G., Lero, D., and LaGrange, A. (2006). Towards a predictive model of quality in Canadian child care centres. *Early Childhood Research Quarterly*, 21(3), 280–295.

Hallam, R., Buell, M. J., and Ridgley, R. (2003). Preparing early childhood educators to serve children and families living in poverty: A national survey of undergraduate programs. *Journal of Research in Childhood Education*, 18(2), 115–124.

Hestenes, L. L., Cassidy, D. J., Hegde, A. V., and Lower, J. K. (2007). Quality in inclusive and noninclusive infant and toddler classrooms. *Journal of Research in Childhood Education*, 22(1), 69–84.

Hock, E., McBride, S., and Gnezda, M. (1989). Maternal separation anxiety: Mother–infant separation from the maternal perspective. *Child Development*, 60(4), 793–802.

Johansson, E. (2004). Learning encounters in preschool: Interaction between atmosphere, view of children and of learning. *International Journal of Early Childhood*, 36(2), 9–26.

Kowalski, H. S., et al. (2005). The long-day childcare context: Implications for toddlers' pretend play. *Early Years: An International Journal of Research and Development*, 25(1), 55–65.

Macfarlane, K., Noble, K., and Cartmel, J. (2004). Pedagogy in the nursery: Establishing practitioner partnerships in high-quality long day care programs. *Australian Journal of Early Childhood*, 29(4), 38–44.

Miller, L., Dalli, C., and Urban, M. (eds.) (2012). *Early childhood grows up: Towards a critical ecology of the profession.* Dordrecht/Heidelberg/London/New York: Springer.

Mitchelmore, S., Degotardi, S., and Fleet, A. (2017). The richness of everyday moments: Bringing visibility to the qualities of care within pedagogical spaces. In E. J. White and C. Dalli (eds.), *Policy and pedagogy with under-three-year olds* (pp. 87–99). Dordrecht. Springer.

Munton, T., Mooney, A., Moss, P., Petrie, P., Clark, A., and Woolner, J. (2002). *Research on ratios, group size and staff qualifications and training in early years and childcare settings.* Research Report No. 320. London: Thomas Coram Research Unit, Institute of Education, University of London.

National Scientific Council on the Developing Child (2004). *Young Children Develop in an Environment of Relationships: Working Paper No. 1.* http://developingchild.harvard.edu/wp-content/uploads/2004/04/Young-Children-Develop-in-an-Environment-of-Relationships.pdf (Accessed on: 14/08/2017).

Nimmo, J., and Park, S. (2009). Engaging early childhood teachers in the thinking and practice of inquiry: Collaborative research mentorship as a tool for shifting teacher identity. *Journal of Early Childhood Teacher Education*, 30(2), 93–104.

OECD. (2016). *PF3.2: Enrolment in Childcare and Pre-school.* OECD Family Database, Social Policy Division, Directorate of Employment, Labour and Social Affairs (Updated: 09.10.16). www.oecd.org/els/soc/PF3_2_Enrolment_childcare_preschool.pdf (Accessed on: 14/08/2017).

Pairman, A. and Dalli, C. (2017). Children creating spaces of care in diverse early childhood centre built environments: A complex interplay of social relations and materiality. In J. Horton and M. Pyer (eds.), *Children, young people and care.* London: Taylor and Francis.

Raikes, H. H., Torquait, J., Hegland, S., Raikes, H., Scott, J., Messner, L. et al (2006). Studying the culture of quality early education and care: A cumulative approach to measuring characteristics of the workforce and relations to quality in four midwestern states. In M. Zaslow (Ed.), *Critical issues in early childhood professional development* (pp. 111–136). Baltimore, MD: Paul H Brookes Publishing.

Rogoff, B., Alcalá, L., Coppens, A. D., López, A., Ruvalcaba, O., and Silva, K. G. (2014). Children learning by observing and pitching-in in their families and community endeavors: An orientation. Special Issue. *Human Development*, 57(2–3), 69–81.

Turp, M. (2006). Why love matters: How affection shapes a baby's brain: A review. *Infant Observation*, 9(3), 305–309.

Valenza, E., Otsuka, Y., Bulf, H., Kanazawa, S., and Yamaguchi, M. (2015). Face orientation and motion differently affect the deployment of visual attention in newborns and 4-month-old infants. *PLoS One*, 10(9), 1–20.

INDEX

activities, creative and cultural: framing of within environments and settings 114; overview of Open Sesame birth-to-twos project 120–123; reflections upon significance of Open Sesame project 129–132; *see also locations of particular e.g.* Hastings Museum and Art Gallery; Jerwood Gallery; Towner Art Gallery

anticipation, relational: importance in practitioner understanding of two-year-olds 64–66; *see also* watchfulness, practitioner

arts activities: overview of Open Sesame birth-to-twos project 120–123; reflections upon significance of Open Sesame project 129–132; *see also locations of particular e.g.* Hastings Museum and Art Gallery; Jerwood Gallery; Towner Art Gallery

assessment: use, role and practices of educational psychologists 135–137

attention, individual: requirement in process of minding 11–13

birth-to-twos: overview of Open Sesame projects 120–123; reflections upon significance of Open Sesame projects 129–132; *see also* two-year-olds; *see also locations of particular projects for e.g.* Hastings Museum and Art Gallery; Jerwood Gallery; Towner Art Gallery

case studies: context and approach of childminder provision 95–96; context

and approach of community preschool provision 96–98; context and approach of rural daycare provision 98–99; context and approach of school nursery unit provision 99–102

Castledon setting: characteristics of activities in 106–107; framing of practitioner-child communication in 113–115; practitioner views on classification within 108–113; uniqueness of setting and pedagogical practices 115–117

challenges and experiences, practitioner: characteristics of 75–82, 88–89

childminders: context and approach to provision for two-year-olds 95–96

children: impact of child risk, vulnerability and resilience on development, perceptions and policies 29–33; implications of critical and sensitive development of 23–26; *see also e.g.* identity, individual; power, practitioner-child; resilience, child; *see also factors enhancing e.g.* attention, individual; early childhood education and care; interactions and experiences, child-adult

classification and framing: of activities within educational settings 108–115; uniqueness of within settings 115–117

communication, practitioner-child: framing of within environments and settings 113–115; uniqueness of within settings 115–117; *see also* listening; *see also tools enhancing e.g.* documentation; *see also*

152 Index

type e.g. interactions and experiences, child-adult

community preschool: context and approach to provision for two-year-olds 96–98

consultation and intervention: use, role and practices of educational psychologists 137–138

contact, families: need for to ensure ECEC quality 45; *see also* interactions and experiences, child-adult; parents

creative and cultural activities: overview of Open Sesame birth-to-twos project 120–123; reflections upon significance of Open Sesame project 129–132; *see also locations of particular e.g.* Hastings Museum and Art Gallery; Jerwood Gallery; Towner Art Gallery

criteria, activities: framing of within environments and settings 114

daycare, rural: context and approach to provision for two-year-olds 98–99

development, child: implications of critical and sensitive periods of 23–26; *see also aspects e.g.* identity, individual; resilience, child; vulnerability, child; *see also factors enhancing e.g.* attention, individual; early childhood education and care

disadvantage (concept): impact on child development, perceptions and government policies 27–28; *see also features ameliorating e.g.* early childhood education and care; policies, governmental

documentation: discourse and descriptions about two-year-olds 55–59

early childhood education and care (ECEC): characteristics of provision 93–95; context and approach of childminder 95–96; context and approach of community preschool 96–98; context and approach of rural daycare 98–99; context and approach of school nursery unit 99–102; historical development 1–3; impact of child personal identity and disadvantage 27–28; impact of child vulnerability, risk and resilience 29–33; overview of policies 37–39; *see also* development, child; environments and settings, ECEC; ethos, pre-school; minds and minding; practitioners; quality, ECEC; two-year-olds

education *see* training

environments and settings, ECEC: activities and aspects enabling satisfactory movement within 108–115; characteristics of educational 106–108; contexts and approaches to provision 93–102; importance of quality and appropriate structures 146–147; importance of supportive governmental policies 147–148; uniqueness of setting and pedagogical practices 115–117; views on quality of 45; *see also players within e.g.* practitioners; two-year-olds

ethos, pre-school: significance for ECEC 67–68

evidence-based approaches: of educational psychologists to their work 138

experiences and challenges, practitioner: characteristics of 75–82, 88–89

externalisation and internalisation: significance in process of child minding 14–16

families: need for connection with to ensure ECEC quality 45; *see also* interactions and experiences, child-adult; parents

figured worlds, pre-school: significance for ECEC 67–68

framing and classification: of activities within educational settings 108–115; uniqueness of within settings 115–117

Hastings Museum and Art Gallery: Open Sesame project at 125–127

identity, individual: development in two-year-olds 26–28

interactions and experiences, child-adult: framing of within environments and settings 114–115; role in child development of understandings of language 51–53; uniqueness of within settings 115–117; *see also* communication, practitioner-child; contact, families; language, personal; power, practitioner-child; *see also aspects influencing e.g.* anticipation, relational; ethos, pre-school; watchfulness, practitioner

internalisation and externalisation: significance in adult-child interactions 14–16

internet: discourse and descriptions of parental roles 58

intersubjectivity: and learning process of minding two-year-olds 11–13

Index

intervention and consultation: use, role and practices of educational psychologists 137–138

Jerwood Gallery (Hastings): Open Sesame project at 123–125

knowledge, practitioner: characteristics of required training 75–79, 81–82, 88–89; importance within work of practitioners 143–146; models and theories 85–88; *see also* preparedness, practitioner

language, personal: and access to shared meanings in process of minding 16–18; relationship with thinking 53–55; *see also* documentation; interactions and experiences, child-adult
listening: importance in deciding educational readiness of two-year-olds 105–106; *see also* communication, practitioner-child; interactions and experiences, child-adult; *see also locations e.g.* environments and settings, ECEC
literature: discourse and descriptions about two-year-olds 55–59

meanings, shared: and personal language in minding of two-year-olds 16–18
minds and minding: impact of child development 23–26; implications affecting process of 18–20; interpretations when caring for two-year-olds 8–11; intersubjectivity and learning of 11–13; significance of internalisation and externalisation 14–16; use of language to access shared meanings in process of 16–18; *see also* policies, governmental; watchfulness, practitioner; *see also types of minding e.g.* early childhood education and care
models and theories: of practitioner knowledge, training and qualifications 85–88

nursery places: impact of child development on provision of 23–26
nursery unit, school: context and approach to provision for two-year-olds 99–102

Open Sesame birth-to-twos project: project overview, purpose and role 120–123; reflections upon significance of 129–132; *see also locations of particular projects e.g.* Hastings Museum and Art Gallery; Jerwood Gallery; Towner Art Gallery

pacing, of activities: framing of within environments and settings 114
parents: targeted documentation describing two-year-olds 57–59; *see also* families; interactions and experiences, child-adult
Parkside setting: characteristics of activities in 107–108; framing of practitioner-child communication in 113–115; practitioner views on classification within 108–113; uniqueness of setting and pedagogical practices 115–117
pedagogy: uniqueness of within settings 115–117
policies, governmental: educational readiness discourses 104–105; implications of child development for 23–26; implications of child identity and disadvantage for 27–28; implications of child vulnerability, risk and resilience for 29–33; importance of supportive ECEC structures 147–148; overview of ECEC 37–39
policy documents: discourse and descriptions of two-year-olds 55–57
politics: educational readiness discourses 104–105
power, practitioner-child: uniqueness within settings 116
practitioners: experiences and challenges 75–82, 88–89; importance of being 'good' with two-year-olds 68–70; role in reducing disadvantage and risk and enhancing child resilience 29–33; views of on practitioner quality 43–45; views of on priorities ensuring ECEC quality 45–47; views on educational environments and settings 108–115; *see also* communication, practitioner-child; early childhood education and care; minds and minding; pedagogy; power, practitioner-child; responses, practitioner; watchfulness, practitioner; *see also aspects influencing role e.g.* anticipation, relational; knowledge, practitioner; policies, governmental; preparedness, practitioner; qualifications, practitioner; responsiveness; training; *see also particular e.g.* psychologists, educational; *see also tools e.g.* creative and cultural activities
preparedness, practitioner: factors ensuring 82–85, 86; *see also elements enabling e.g.* knowledge, practitioner; qualifications, practitioner; training

154 Index

preschools: context and approach to provision for two-year-olds 96–98

psychologists, educational: assessment role 135–137; consultation and intervention role 137–138; evidence-based approaches of 138; supervision role 139; training support role 139–140

qualifications, practitioner: characteristics of required 75–79, 81–82; models and theories 85–88; *see also* preparedness, practitioner

quality, ECEC: debates surrounding 39–42; importance for ECEC environments 146–147; stakeholder views for aspects and priorities ensuring 43–47; understanding quality of for two-year-olds provision 42–43; *see also factors affecting e.g.* ethos, pre-school; knowledge, practitioner; preparedness, practitioner; qualifications, practitioner; watchfulness, practitioner

readiness, educational: discourses on 104–105; importance of listening to child 105–106

resilience, child: impact on child development, perceptions and government policies 29–33

responses, practitioner: need to guarantee in work with two-year-olds 72; *see also* interactions and experiences, child-adult; *see also factors affecting e.g.* watchfulness, practitioner

responsiveness: importance within work of practitioners 143–146

risk, child: impact on child development, perceptions and government policies 29–33

rural daycare: context and approach to provision for two-year-olds 98–99

sequencing, of activities: framing of within environments and settings 114

stress, child: importance of reduction of within ECEC 146–147

structures, ECEC: essentiality of appropriate 146–147

supervision: use, role and practices of educational psychologists 139

teaching: uniqueness of within settings 115–117

theories and models: of practitioner knowledge, training and qualifications 85–88

thinking: relationship with language 53–55

Towner Art Gallery (Eastbourne): Open Sesame project at 127–129

training: characteristics of required practitioner 75–79, 81–82; models and theories of 85–88; support role and practices of educational psychologists 139–140; *see also* preparedness, practitioner

Treetops setting: characteristics of activities in 108; framing of practitioner-child communication in 113–115; practitioner views on classification within 108–113; uniqueness of setting and pedagogical practices 115–117

two-year-olds: context and approach of childminder provision 95–96; context and approach of community preschool provision 96–98; context and approach of rural daycare provision 98–99; context and approach of school nursery unit provision 99–102; descriptions in literature 55–59; evolution of understandings of language through interaction 51–53; impact of critical and sensitive periods of development 23–26; impact of personal identity and disadvantage 27–28; impact of vulnerability, risk and resilience of 29–33; implications for minding of 18–20; importance of listening to in deciding educational readiness 105–106; importance of relational anticipation for understanding of 64–66; interpretations of minding process when caring for 8–11; intersubjectivity and learning to mind 11–13; relationship between language with thinking of 53–55; significance of internalisation and externalisation in minding 14–16; *see also* birth-to-twos; *see also factors affecting care of e.g.* environments and settings, ECEC; ethos, pre-school; policies, governmental; practitioners; quality, ECEC

vulnerability, child: impact on child development, perceptions and government policies 29–33

watchfulness, practitioner: importance of need to value 70–72; ways of ensuring in work with two-year-olds 72

workforce, ECEC *see* practitioners